Mosquito

Classic Aircraft No.7: Their history and how to model them

Michael J.F. Bowyer and Bryan Philpott

PSL Patrick Stephens, Cambridge

First published in 1980

British Library Cataloguing in Publication Data

Bowyer, Michael John Frederick
   Mosquito. — (Classic aircraft; no.7).
   1. Mosquito (Bombers)
   2. Airplanes — Models
   I. Title II. Philpott, Bryan III. Series
   623.74'63   TL686.D4

ISBN 0 85059 432 4

Photoset in 9 on 10 pt English Times by
Industrial Artists (Hitchin) Ltd, Hitchin, Herts.
Printed in Great Britain on 115 gsm Nimrod coated
cartridge, and bound, by The Garden City Press,
Letchworth, for the publishers, Patrick Stephens
Limited, Bar Hill, Cambridge, CB3 8EL, England.

Contents

Introduction

There can surely be no doubt that the de Havilland Mosquito remains the most cost-effective aeroplane of all time. None other has shown such ubiquity.

This was a private venture for which the Air Ministry had no use. Many in high places disbelieved its originators, failing to recognise the farsightedness of its birth.

This was an aeroplane which, from the moment that it commenced action, proved supreme. Faster than many a Spitfire, able to fly higher than almost any other operational aircraft, as potent when engaging night raiders as when it was bombing Berlin — and it daylight; this was the Mosquito.

Drawing upon amply available supplies of wood, a material of great strength and so easily repairable, the Mosquito brought into the war effort in a most important manner many industries hitherto unemployed during the Second World War.

Within the last year of conflict this small aeroplane, cheap to produce, cheap to run and needing far less in manpower than others, mounted a hard-hitting and highly accurate bombing campaign almost without loss. Added to this was the quite amazing ability it had to roam at will across Europe in daylight bringing back some of the most spectacular photographs of all time, while others of its species maintained a vital diplomatic and intelligence link with neutral Sweden.

By the end of hostilities Mosquitoes were frequently flying six-hour sorties at very high speeds, and when armed with rockets and guns were as effective as any fighter-bombers of the warring nations.

Strange, then, that the Mosquito has never won its rightful place in public esteem. The reasons for this are varied. One is that it was not an aeroplane of the Establishment, another the great secrecy that surrounded it for much of its active life, mainly because it was born in wartime. Many of its amazingly successful operations had to remain cloaked in secrecy, whether it be releasing patriots from Gestapo torture or protecting the RAF's night bombers. To popular mind it remains the Hurricane, Lancaster and Spitfire that won the RAF immortal fame. The Mosquito eclipsed them all.

Acknowledgements

The material upon which this book is based has been derived from a wide number of sources. It is drawn from the records of the famous de Havilland Aircraft Company of Hatfield which became part of Hawker Siddeley and has now lost its identity to become part of British Aerospace. To three organisations we are therefore indebted for assistance, and particularly to Vernon W. Clarkson of the Chester Division of British Aerospace.

Of the team which at Hatfield produced and promoted the Mosquito my memories will ever linger for they were exceptionally gifted, talented people with whom to have worked was indeed a privilege. For their past help I am extremely grateful, and in particular for having been guided through the great days of the Mosquito some years ago by Martin C. Sharp.

We are deeply indebted to the many occasions in the past when help with the Mosquito story was afforded by the heads of staff of the Ministry of Defence (Air Historical Branch) and Ministry of Aviation (now Ministry of Defence PE), many of whose records and files are now lodged in the Public Record Office. To the Keeper of the Public Record Office we are grateful for permission to reproduce certain diagrams. The drawings in Part One are by Laurence J. Haylock.

I am indebted to the following for the use of photographs: E.C. Armées; de Havilland/Hawker Siddeley Aviation/British Aerospace; R.H. Finlayson; B.T. Gibbins; Imperial War Museum; Gunnar A. Lindaas; Dave Menard; John D.R. Rawlings; Rolls-Royce; M.J. Smith and Kyle Webster. **M.J.F.B.**

I should like to express my sincere thanks to the following people and organisations without whose help it would not have been possible for me to contribute the modelling section to this book:

Stuart Howe of the Mosquito Museum, Malcolm Parr of British Airways European Division, G. J. Hales of A. A. Hales Ltd, Barry Wheeler of Airfix Products Ltd, G. J. Seagrave of Revell (GB) Ltd, Maurice Landi of Lesney Bros Ltd, Tony Woollet, Tom Cope, John Carter and other members of the Reading Branch IPMS, IPMS UK, IPMS USA, IPMS Canada, IPMS Australasia, Trents Model Shops, the Newbury Police Modelling Club, the British Aerospace Aircraft Group Chester, in particular Mr V. W. Clarkson who very patiently answered a host of letters and supplied extremely helpful drawings.

Thanks are also due to Richard Leask Ward, who provided most of the drawings as well as his usual authoritative and unselfish assistance, Bruce Robertson, Mike Bowyer, and Charles King. **B.P.**

Chapter One

'It'll never work!'

Simple in concept, superb in battle, the most effective military aircraft of all time. This was the Mosquito, its successful fighting career based on a design which was doctrinally opposed to that of its predecessors. Born of an idea derided by officialdom, and within a concern whose excellence carried it to a superlative position in the world's aircraft industry, the Mosquito was no outcome of a string of committee meetings. Great aeroplanes seldom are. Here was private venture and initiative, blocked by government stubborness, at its very best.

De Havilland had, decades previously, concluded that speed in a bomber was a better means of defence than guns. He had evolved the DH4, with this notion in mind, during the First World War. Yet it was not to be with military aircraft that the company would achieve wide acclaim after that conflict. Captain Geoffrey de Havilland, and the team which he attracted, were all dedicated to the advancement of flying for civilian purposes; for mass travel and, particularly, for sporting pleasures.

De Havilland, later to become Sir Geoffrey, was deeply interested in wildlife and, in particular lepidoptera. His ventures were frequently to Africa to view at first hand the most impressive creatures on earth. He was not only an avid collector and recorder of wildlife scenes, he was indeed a skilled painter. Long hanging in the de Havilland Directors' meeting place (on the St Albans road leading from Hatfield) was a most magnificent painting of a lioness, proving his talent.

He, and those who worked with him, were peaceful people to whom the thought that aeroplanes were for war was anathema. One might reasonably conclude that a desire to maintain peace and retain a free society must drive such people to defend that which they hold when trouble threatens. Little wonder that, when the skies over Europe began to darken in the late 1930s, the unsurpassed talent at Hatfield was caused to consider what contribution this famed team could make to the defence of Britain.

Since the end of the 1914-18 war de Havilland aeroplanes had performed well in mixed transport roles. Mostly, they were biplanes. Whilst the Royal Air Force bought some, mainly for training or light transport duties, most de Havilland sales were to flying clubs and small air lines. Experiences in the 1920s had made the company wary of government schemes. Almost without exception their aircraft were to achieve success and

general superiority over contenders, so much so that de Havilland aeroplanes of the 1930s are still about in some number.

No de Havilland design of the 1930s was to capture public excitement more dramatically than the DH88 Comet racer. Its speed of conception and construction were remarkable, particularly for such a radical design. Retracting undercarriage and variable pitch propellers made it seem very advanced for its time. Superb streamlined shape and aesthetically appealing form made it tremendously exciting to gaze upon. Even these attributes were out-shone when Comet G-ACSS spectacularly won the Mildenhall-Melbourne Air Race of 1934. This event, which attracted some very advanced aircraft of that period including the metal DC-2 and Boeing 247, both pacemaking airliners, was to result in what must surely be the most superb military aeroplane of all time, the Mosquito. The path by which that aeroplane became reality, though, was to be tortuous and much delayed by disbelief.

Within days of the Comet's success de Havilland had roughed out plans for an airliner based upon the racer. This, too, would be of wooden construction and would rely upon four de Havilland Gipsy engines. It would be able to carry a 1,000 lb payload across the Atlantic, thus becoming the company's first North Atlantic mail carrier. Alas, necessary government support was lacking. Plans so enthusiastically devised were ministerially drowned. De Havilland received the sort of reception all too often afforded to the talented of Britain.

Already the RAF Expansion Scheme of the mid-1930s

Star performer, the DH 88 Comet racer G-ACSS shown at the 1951 Festival of Britain exhibition on the South Bank.

had been publicly announced. De Havilland was eager to participate but the question was how could the company provide for the Service anything other than wooden trainers and light transports? The answer partly came in August 1936.

The Air Staff had decided that the new breed of monoplane bombers for the RAF would need to be replaced in 1940 by aircraft considered ideal for Bomber Command. There would first be the B.1/35 medium bomber to be eventually supplanted by a much superior design based upon Specification P.13/36 supported by a smaller number of large four-engined bombers.

It was the P.13/36 requirements circulated in August 1936 which aroused interest at Hatfield. A two-engined medium bomber was needed for worldwide service, one in which the inter-play of range, speed and bomb load, heightened in each case by assisted take-off, could be most usefully exploited. A high cruising speed would ensure that the aircraft spent as little time as possible over enemy territory. The crew would number four or six, and nose and tail turrets were specified. A range of 3,000 miles was needed, a top speed of 275 mph at 15,000 feet and a bomb load of 4,000 lb. To complicate matters the Air Ministry suggested that the design should be capable of adaptation to the roles of medium bomber, general reconnaissance or general purpose. For good measure it should also be able to carry two torpedoes, a quixotic feature popularly tucked into bomber requirements of the late 1930s.

De Havilland contemplated the possibility of adapting their Albatross mail plane. Calculations suggested that with two engines such a 36,000 lb bomber would have an economical cruise speed of 275 mph at 15,000 ft, and after catapult launching would achieve the 3,000-mile range required.

In keeping with the other DH designs of the period the DH91 Albatross would be of wooden construction, and this was proposed for its bomber derivative. The company was ever ready to point out, then and later, that steel-Dural-spruce had similar strength/weight ratios, that wood skinning gave a very smooth finish and that — other than in a torsion plane — wood was as strong as steel.

During 1936 and 1937 the company became much involved with the DH91. In the future there would be the DH94 Moth Minor lightplane which it was hoped would succeed the Tiger Moth. There was to be a new high-speed, twin-engined airliner, the appealingly shaped DH95 Flamingo. Therefore, although the company wanted to play a first line part in the RAF Expansion Scheme, it did have considerable work in hand. In any case, tenders for P.13/36 were awarded without de Havilland's somewhat restrained contender obtaining much interest.

Nevertheless, the company considered forthcoming likely bomber requirements and produced schemes for twin-engined DH91 variants powered either by Hercules, Sabre or Merlin engines. By July 1938, favour had fallen upon the latter — de Havilland always had discriminating good taste. The company contacted the Air Ministry asking for time to work out their ideas for an improved medium bomber. Their calculations suggested that to meet the 13/36 specification an aircraft would need a very high wing loading. Indeed, that it could not be met by a twin-engined aircraft. Provision for assisted take-off would mean specially stressing the machine, thus causing excessive wing loading. To reach the required speed the machine would be able to carry only half of the specified load. An aircraft larger than required would, in de Havilland's opinion, emerge with a maximum speed of about 212 mph at 15,000 ft. Events proved this contention, but for very different reasons.

The DH 91 Albatross air liner played an important part in Mosquito evolution (de Havilland).

The Halifax four-engined bomber was born out of Handley-Page's contender to P.13/36 and to be acceptable had to have a four-engined configuration. The other design, the Avro Manchester, suffered pitifully from un-developed Vulture engines as a result of which it, too, emerged four-engined as the Lancaster.

De Havilland's calculations suggested that their twin-Merlin bomber would have a 1,500-mile range when carrying a 4,000 lb bomb load — half that required by P.13/36. Its top speed should be about 260 mph at 19,000 ft, and it would cruise at around 230 mph. But to meet all demands of 13/36, double the power would be needed and possibly Napier Sabres, at which point that dreaded spectre of the mid-1930s, a prohibitively long take-off, came into prospect.

It was now that de Havilland came along with a compromise suggestion. Many specifications of the period listed 'standard equipment' which to de Havilland appeared to be of very questionable value. They suggested that many of these items could be deleted thus improving the operational height of their bomber. Whilst considering their P.13/36 contender the company also looked at the possibility of producing a twin-Gipsy engined light general purpose aircraft fitted with one nose gun and two tail guns. Clearly, such a machine would become far more potent if Merlin-powered — which brought back the preferred line of development.

Even after removing all the questionable equipment from their bomber, de Havilland considered that a top speed of little over 300 mph at 20,000 ft would be attained. The barrier to greatly increased speed was clearly the weight of turreted armament.

It was in October 1938 that a completely new concept came into being, an unarmed bomber with fighter speed. Such a machine would be small, carry a hefty offensive load, fly high, have a two-man crew and be of wooden construction. The latter was chosen because it would not only confer a smooth finish but also because wood, in the event of war, would be in ample supply.

The Munich crisis of September 1938 heightened de Havilland's desire to make a really worthwhile contribution to arming the RAF. Therefore Captain Geoffrey de Havilland and Charles Walker went to the Air Ministry to discuss their radical idea.

They met considerable scepticism among Ministry officials, people not readily given to entertaining radicalism and certainly not when it was propounded by a concern which had shunned becoming too much involved with government notions. In any case, the bomber programme for the 1940s was set and being implemented. The notion of an unarmed high-speed bomber was turned down.

De Havilland was now much occupied with a new all-metal airliner, the DH95 Flamingo. Consideration was given to whether this might possibly evolve into a bomber heavily armed to suit the out-dated official thinking. It would carry four 500 lb bombs and feature a nosewheel undercarriage. Its top speed would be about 280 mph TAS at 17,000 ft, service ceiling 24,000 ft and for the three-man crew oxygen would be carried for a seven-hour flight in a aeroplane quite divorced from what de Havilland really wanted to build.

As an improvement upon the initial DH95 bomber scheme, consideration was given to installing Bristol Taurus radials whose cross-section was decreased by 6 in thus reducing drag, although it was forecast that these new engines might become quite heavy. True, they were expected to need less fuel, but the final estimate of a top speed of around 285 mph made the scheme unattractive.

During the initial stages of DH95 involvement in a bomber scheme, de Havilland received an invitation to tender to Specification B.18/38 for a bomber utilising non-strategic materials which were to be wedded to a steel foundation. This the company viewed as a half-hearted notion, possibly stemming from a lack of courage to build wooden front-line aircraft when all those around were built of metal. The performance required by B.18/38 was far from exciting, and again it would be packed with an astonishing assortment of use-less items.

Since October 1938, de Havilland had worked upon their radical unarmed proposition under the designation 'DH98 Reconnaissance-Bomber' and a proliferation of DH95 modified designs were now being considered. Clearly, the stumbling block to high performance was the weighty gun turret. One forward turret and a crew of three for the aircraft was considered, then a tail turret. In every case a mediocre bomber with a top speed of about 260 mph seemed a likely outcome once operational equipment was added. But, take away all the turrets, reduce the crew to two and the result was totally different, completely desirable. Keep the aircraft small, reduce the crew to two, build of wood for strength and rapid battle damage repair and fit powerful engines. Then the longed for 'Ideal Bomber — DH edition' would be achieved. Why, it was argued, train gunners for an aircraft designed not to fight but to drop bombs? The saving in production capacity would be enormous, the training programmes vastly cheaper. The operational effectiveness? Vastly greater — and there was the possibility of a very long-range, even four-engined variant. Such bombers would be exposed to enemy interference for relatively brief periods and on account of their speed be able to deliver bomb loads faster. They would surely have a far superior service-ability record than more complicated aircraft. The success of such aircraft, such a concept, must rest upon one aspect; they would *have* to fly faster than any enemy fighter.

De Havilland pressed these ideas whenever the chance occurred, but official opinion questioned the validity of them. The great, nagging fear was that the enemy would evolve a fighter faster than this new bomber. To order bomber crews into action in undefended aircraft was something that was unacceptable to officers brought up on the thinking of the 1920s and '30s (and some even with First World War experience). Behind the ministerial doors there was a very different concern. This new bomber needed Merlin engines. These were already totally committed to the front-line fighter force, and it looked as if bombers already being developed might need them in increasing numbers. There was just not available a further Merlin production source for a further bomber project. It was this aspect as much as any other that made it impossible to proceed with the DH98.

As Europe slid towards conflict de Havilland, to so many the premier British aircraft company, was building wooden trainers and a few airliners whose future, to say the least, was doubtful. Such was the state when war broke out on that warm, cloudy Sunday in September 1939.

At once Geoffrey de Havilland decided he must press the fast bomber. He went again to the Ministry to propose once more the basic ideas for an unarmed bomber which could come home unscathed — even, if necessary, from Berlin itself.

It is easy to understand how unlikely such a possibility must have seemed, to both Air Ministry and the Air Staff. They already possessed, and in profusion, examples of a bomber that would 'fly faster than fighters'. In that case, however, they were aged biplane fighters. And as for a crew of two — could they cope? But at least there was no outright rejection of the ideas. Other manufacturers had, it was discovered, been working upon small, fast bomber designs, perhaps after hearing of the de Havilland plans. Short Bros for instance had opted for an air-launched machine using the Mayo Composite principle. Meanwhile the de Havilland team now began looking in earnest at the ideal layout for their aircraft.

They opted for a bomber with a wing span of about 50 ft. After much deliberation they chose the already trustworthy Merlin, although new engines like the very powerful Sabre might, despite their weight, confer faster speed. Such power plants could be used for later variants of the aircraft. A cruising speed of around 330 mph was aimed at with, it was hoped, a top speed of over 400 mph. A bomb load of 1,000 lb would be carried fast and a combat radius of 750 miles achieved. The performance liability of a tail turret was forecast in case the Ministry refused to agree to a design which lacked such a penalising contraption. It would have reduced the payload by about 500 lb, and the speed by a crucial 20 mph at least. To this needed to be added the weight of the necessary crew member and ammunition — as well as additional structure — so that the overall penalty was considerable, the top speed falling dramatically by about 60 mph.

There was, however, no reason why the airframe could not be adapted for a special reconnaissance role. The need for a fast photographic-reconnaissance aircraft was very apparent at this time. Blenheims of 2 Group and the AASF were busy photographing Germany on quite a considerable scale, but the crews were having some alarming experiences and losses were being suffered. This new de Havilland machine would have been ideal for the task. Even more important, its range would permit it to be used for maritime fighter patrol and convoy escort duties. The addition of cannon and machine guns would be a relatively straightforward matter. Modified in this manner, such a machine would make an ideal long-endurance day and night fighter, a role for which the Beaufighter was the only type envisaged and whose production rate looked problematical, tied up as it was with the demand for more Beaufort torpedo bombers.

Detailed design investigations were presented to the Air Ministry in November. The company stressed just how much effect a tail turret would have upon the aircraft's quality. It was therefore decided that no turret be fitted although, for a long time, there remained a desire for fixed scare guns to be installed either below the rear fuselage or in the rear of the nacelles. Very careful checks on the drag of turrets were ordered as a double check, and wooden models of the DH98 design were wind tunnel tested at Farnborough.

In December there were new shock waves when Bomber Command officers stated that they had no place in their Command for an unarmed bomber. Their scepticism was more than confirmed when a force of heavily armed Wellingtons was shot down. The chance of a safe return for a lonely reconnaissance aircraft would surely lessen — but if this new machine could fly fast and high the Command agreed there then might be a place for it. There were more discussions by which time Air Chief Marshal Sir Wilfred Freeman KCB, DSO, MC, Air Member for Development and Production, had become fully won over by the project and now championed its cause. At last de Havilland had a good friend in the best possible position.

At the close of 1939 it was decided to draw up an official specification for a fast, unarmed bomber/reconnaissance aircraft. Its all-up weight would be around 17,000-18,000 lb, and it would be powered by two Rolls-Royce Merlins. Its top speed would be close to 400 mph at about 23,000 ft. It would cruise at about 330 mph at 27,000 ft and its range would be about 1,500 miles. These figures seemed phenomenal.

On March 1 1940 a contract was concluded for 50 examples of the aircraft including the prototype. This most important aeroplane would be built in a newly erected building at Salisbury Hall where the de Havilland design team had been moved when an order for the DH98 seemed likely. On this dispersal site the project would be safer from possible enemy air attack. Now the site is the home of the Mosquito Museum, a 'Mosquito Mecca'.

Thus, the project, so hardly fought for, so radical in concept, would become reality — and soon. But what would this advanced machine be called? What is small, gives a death bite and does so over a wide area? The exact moment when 'Mosquito' was chosen will probably never be now known.

Chapter Two

The prelude

The contract secured, the name chosen, now the task was production. De Havilland approached well known furniture makers whose war work was hitherto limited. At High Wycombe, Gommes, makers of 'G Plan' furniture, would build tailplanes. Dancer & Hearne would become involved with Mosquito building, like Mulliners of Chiswick. Production would by the summer of 1940 also start at the Second Aircraft Group, Western Avenue.

Just as those plans were being activated it was the newly devised Ministry of Aircraft Production who now took a turn at trying to axe the Mosquito. After the fall of France a re-appraisal of all aircraft projects came about, as a result of which it was decided to concentrate on producing and developing five main types. Materials would be diverted to these — yet what of the unwanted wooden miracle? Three times Lord Beaverbrook ordered work to be halted on the Mosquito, but no executive instruction was ever received at Hatfield. The Mosquito did not make much demand upon strategic materials and so it survived, only just, in part because of a promise to deliver 50 to the RAF by July 1941.

During that most beautiful summer of 1940, when to be alive was to be chancing fate whilst being much moved by the historical adventure unfolding, the building of the prototype proceeded, under great secrecy, at Salisbury Hall. Looking back to those days it

never ceases to amaze me just how much leaked out about the secret aircraft — and that de Havilland were engaged upon a high-speed bomber was common knowledge. Maybe the Germans never believed rumours, unlike the handful of aviation enthusiasts of the day who, upon past evidence, viewed rumour as all but gospel!

By the end of the first week of August 1940 the second Mosquito fuselage shell was complete and the wing skinning was about to be produced by Vanden Plas at Hendon. At Hatfield, metal parts were being cut. Seven fuselage shells had been built by mid-September yet the enemy seemed unaware of what was creeping up on him. . . or did he? On October 3 1940 a Junkers 88 of KG 77 set off from Laon to bomb a biscuit factory in Reading. Visibility was poor and the crew failed to find their target. They set course easterly, coming across the Hatfield works. Two runs and bombs had destroyed 80 per cent of the machined parts, killed 21 people, wounded 70 but missed the much-dispersed Mosquito main assemblies. Small arms fire brought down the raider. There would be a setback to production and, more important, some familiar faces at Hatfield were now but memory. These losses brought greater determination to deal efficiently with the foe.

That day came nearer at the start of November 1940 when, under tarpaulin security wraps, the main

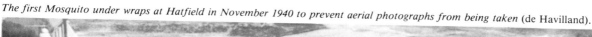

The first Mosquito under wraps at Hatfield in November 1940 to prevent aerial photographs from being taken (de Havilland).

assemblies of the prototype were brought on lorries to Hatfield. There the components were wedded and the engines installed.

Three weeks later came one of the great moments in British aviation when, late on the afternoon of November 25 and with the great de Havilland personalities on the airfield, young Geoffrey de Havilland took E0234, the yellow prototype, on its maiden flight. He returned to tell that all was well, very well, with the beautiful aeroplane.

It had a trade mark, as did nearly all de Havilland aeroplanes — and that was the specially curvaceous fin and rudder. De Havilland were a proud, professional, personal firm, and with good reason. How much we need such excellence nowadays.

During December the prototype flew on most days, but on the ground its bright colour could have been easily detected by nosy foreigners. Therefore, when at rest, it lay outside its hangar shrouded by tarpaulins.

By mid-December 1940 14 fuselage shells had been built, but wing production was lagging and only 16 units were under construction. There really were no problems, but furniture manufacturers had to learn to work to very fine tolerances, use glues carefully and make certain that every fraction of an ounce of unnecessary weight should be machined away.

In London civil servants were enjoying themselves with their forecasts, documents, contracts and calculations. The cost of the first 50 Mosquitoes would be £600,000. De Havilland were told that there was a war on, and that they must not grasp excess profits. Their allowance was finally settled at a meagre 1.75 per cent of the selling price of each Mosquito, some £300 per aircraft.

Mosquito development problems were almost nonexistent, although there can never be any denying that it was an aeroplane demanding utmost respect from its crew. During December 1940 some blistering on the cowling's metal skinning was noticed but not taken much account of, yet it was to plague the aeroplane for a very long time. More noticeable was the fact that a senior Canadian Minister came to Britain at the suggestion of de Havilland (Canada) and late in December he watched a glittering Mosquito display. The following day de Havilland were told that 150 more Mosquitoes would soon be ordered, the contract coming at a vital period in the aircraft's career.

Although it had been decided in November 1940 that

Left Orthochromatic film causes the all-yellow prototype to appear black instead of yellow over-all. Here it wears its original E-0234 identity (IWM).

Below Famed W4050 gets airborne for a test flight on January 10 1941 (de Havilland).

a fighter version should proceed, de Havilland preferred the Mosquito to be built as a bomber. The agreement to have Mosquitoes in Bomber Command had, however, been on the understanding that they would serve as reconnaissance aircraft. So it was that in January 1941 de Havilland were informed that the first prototype would be followed by a photo-reconnaissance aircraft W4051, a prototype fighter W4052 and that the succeeding 19 would be PR Mk 1s and the remainder of the first 50 would be fighters. Bombers, the company was told, would be featured within the next 150 machines. January 1941 witnessed the completion of the first production wing for a PR aircraft, 20 such wings now being underway.

Camouflaging of the prototype came about in February 1941, and in the third week of that month it proceeded to Boscombe Down for initial, official handling trials. Its maximum speed was reckoned by de Havilland to be about 386 mph. The only problems which the prototype had met was some juddering of the tailplane due to the air flow streaming off the much pointed rear engine nacelles, and castoring trouble with the tailwheel. Neither was considered serious.

The Mosquito arrived at Boscombe Down on a

Wednesday. Hatfield's eager team found nothing to enhance their confidence in officials, for the little-moved Boscombe recipients of the precious aeroplane promptly locked it away from the de Havilland men. By lunchtime the civilians were speechless. On Wednesday there was the traditional sports afternoon, so the Mosquito had to wait until next day to perform. And perform it did, much to de Havilland disgust, on Boscombe's scales for a weighing session.

When it eventually flew there was total disbelief at the performance of this wooden contrivance. Cross checks were made repeatedly, the words of the de Havilland men being treated with utmost suspicion. But, it was true. This aeroplane, with two heavy engines and twice the wetted area of a Spitfire, could out-pace that master-piece by over 20 mph, achieving this when flying much higher, at about 22,000 ft. To the amazement of the de Havilland team one official nastily told them that they should have informed his department much sooner about this aircraft. Other paper engineers hurried from London and Farnborough, expressing similar sentiments. All was going brilliantly.

It was late daylight on February 24 1941 when W4050 was taxying across Boscombe Down and the tailwheel

Right *Taxiing at Hatfield, W4050 in January 1941 a few weeks before its back was broken — whilst taxiing (de Havilland).*

Below *The second Mosquito, W4051, served as the PR 1 prototype and, fitted with a production fuselage, flew 14 operational sorties with the PRU before joining 521 (Met) Squadron (de Havilland).*

caught in a rut. That mere castoring trouble struck — and disastrously — for the rear fuselage fractured. Sir Geoffrey de Havilland, Charles Walker and Richard Clarkson were aghast. Surely this was bound to kill the wondrous machine? But not at all. When Sir William Farren DTD, met them, he told them not to worry for they could soon right the trouble. He had now to admit that they had devised a winner. Farren, in months past, had been far from a Mosquito supporter yet here, at last, even he was eulogising over the superb aeroplane. Within a week the fuselage of the second prototype, the PR 1 W4051, had been delivered to Boscombe Down and flown, proving how easy it would be to repair a Mosquito. There had also been a curious twist of events involved, for the second prototype would now have to be fitted with a production-type reconnaissance fuselage and would become one of the few prototypes ever to fly operationally.

It would be untrue to state that the Mosquito encountered no design, production or service problems. The cockpit was packed with instruments and crew, too tightly some said. Getting out in an emergency would always be a problem. In the factories there were moments when getting the aeroplanes glued properly proved difficult. But meanwhile the prototype climbed fast and high, had a top speed of about 392 mph TAS at 22,000 ft and a likely service ceiling of 34,000 ft. It was highly manoeuvrable and a delight to handle.

W4050 was to be the subject of many aerodynamic trials all intended to give a slight improvement, but never over many years would the basic structure and outline change. That indeed is the hallmark of only the finest aeroplanes. Ejector exhausts were found to boost the speed, but cowling blistering problems would remain. To discover what would happen if a dorsal turret was fitted W4050 featured such a mock-up aft of the canopy. This reduced TAS by about 20 mph and generally hindered performance.

The need for a dorsal turret had arisen from the decision to forge ahead with the fighter. A requirement for a long range night and escort fighter, F.18/40, had

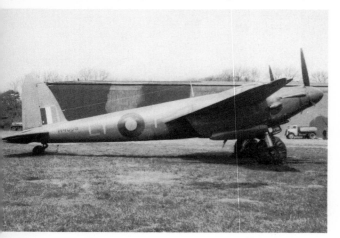

been issued in October 1940. Three months earlier de Havilland had been asked to prepare a fighter Mosquito. Their scheme was now accepted for 18/40, whose role would be to intercept the Condor annoyance over the Atlantic. Fitting four machine-guns and four cannon would do little to alter the Mosquito's performance, but placing the four machine-guns in a turret would reduce the speed from 382 mph to 370 mph, according to estimates. A turret afforded more operational flexibility, but at some cost. Endurance would fall below five hours. Eventually the turret idea was dropped. Two such fighters, W4053 and W4073, had both been flown out of the field adjacent to Salisbury Hall for tests from Hatfield.

Before daybreak on May 13 1941, with the Mosquito fighter two days away from flying out of Salisbury Hall's field, a German spy, Karel Richter, parachuted from a He 111 and landed close to the site. For two days he lay low burying his parachute and trying to organise himself. Richter was no James Bond and soon fell into deep trouble when a lorry driver asked him the way. Richter could not help. The driver than asked P.C. Scott, and made reference to the strange fellow he had just met. Scott found him and took Richter to the police station were the truth emerged, as a result of which Richter was executed in December 1941. Had he lain low a little longer he would have been rewarded well for, in the still of the evening of May 15 young Geoffrey de Havilland flew the all-black W4052 out of Salibury Hall's grounds despite their sloping run of a mere 450 yards. It was a typically courageous and confident effort. Five days later W4052, distinguished partly by having a larger tailplane featured by fighter Mosquitoes, was firing its cannon at the Hatfield butts.

The first photo-reconnaissance aircraft W4051 was following fast on the heels of the fighter and was ready for flight trials on May 24, the day the first production PR 1 W4054 entered the paint shop, which meant that the PR 1 would be first to fly an operational sortie. So eager to try the aircraft was the PRU at Benson that its commander flew W4051 even before Boscombe pilots had approved it. The only problem encountered was engine cutting at high levels on warm days, and it took some refinement to rectify this. Meanwhile the fighter was being taken through its paces and turned in a top speed of 378 mph whilst showing itself sensitive to changes in the centre of gravity which would be important if variations in fuel and weapon loads took their likely courses. Airborne interception radar was installed during August, and various types of exhaust stacks tried, whilst camera fits and fuel consumption featured in the tests of the PR 1s.

The operational debut of the Mosquito was approach-

Mosquito PR 1 W4059 PR Blue over-all with Medium Sea Grey codes and black serial. W4059 flew 59 operational sorties with PRU Benson before joining 540 Squadron and, later, 8 Operational Training Unit before being struck off charge on September 20 1944 (IWM).

Trial installation of the Rolls-Royce Merlin 72 in W4057, the Mosquito Bomber Prototype. Photographed on August 10 1942 (de Havilland).

ing. On July 13 1941 W4051 touched down at Benson. It had taken only eight months since the prototype flew, to achieve this milestone. By September, three Mosquitoes were on the strength of 1 PRU Benson, where the pilots found them much to their liking. It must, however, be said that, in some quarters, there was mistrust during those advanced days, of a wooden throwback. Surely, everyone made aeroplanes out of metal by 1941? Only when the ability of wood to absorb tremendous damage, and the ease with which it could be patched — even using the leg of a bureaucrat's chair — were fully demonstrated, did acceptance come.

Fitting cameras into aircraft for reconnaissance purposes is not the simple matter one might assume. There are often lens and window misting problems, camera heating and film transport to arrange, not to mention the need for minimum vibration and accurate camera settings. By mid-September some of these problems were sorted out sufficiently to allow the great event. Mid-morning on September 17 1941 Squadron Leader Clerke set off in W4055 for a photographic mission to Brest and the Franco-Spanish border. Electrical trouble of the type which can easily ruin an otherwise satifactory flight upset the working of the cameras on this first operation, but the aircraft performed excellently.

There was no need to hold back now. When the weather and serviceability permitted it, Mosquitoes would roam widely and, in particular, over Norway from a detachment based at Wick and later at Leuchars. Performance figures for the PR Mk 1 showed it to have a top speed of about 384 mph TAS at 22,000 ft. These figures were little different for the long-range version carrying extra fuel load, and also for the tropicalised examples.

If one wishes to be pedantic, then W4050 was not strictly a bomber, more an aerodynamic test-bed. The first true bomber was W4057 completed in September 1941 and looked upon as the Mk V prototype. In retrospect it is surely nothing short of amazing that an aeroplane intended to be a bomber should appear as a fighter and fast reconnaissance aircraft before emerging in its primary role. It was not until July 1941 that de Havilland received the go-ahead to build bombers, and then it was for only ten examples, conversions of the last ten PR 1s which then became known as PRU/Bomber Conversion type and later carried the designation B Mk IV srs i.

After Boscombe Down trials W4057 returned to Hatfield for a variety of ground tests, among them an attempt to double its possible bomb load and fit four 500 lb GP bombs. The problem lay in the length of the tail fins of these bombs. The late C.T. Wilkins hit upon the idea of making the bomb fins telescopic, a common feature of iron bombs nowadays but then quite startling.

W4072, the last of the ten PRU/Bomber Conversion Type aircraft also known as B Mk IV srs i. Finish is Dark Green and Dark Earth with Sky under surfaces. Served as GB:D with 105 Squadron, at 1655 Mosquito Training Unit and joined 627 Squadron as AZ:Q in December 1943. Crashed in the sea near Bradwell Bay returning from Frankfurt on January 9 1944 (IWM).

The accepted alternative was to shorten the bomb vanes. The ballistics of the bombs remained good so this idea, the simpler one, proceeded.

Since it was only a matter of converting well advanced PR airframes it was still possible to get the bomber version into service before the fighters came along. For the latter the order would now clearly be very large. There was a suggestion in 1941 of equipping 20 of them with dual controls — useful for training — but the urgency of using the aircraft operationally resulted in only six of the first W serial batch being thus completed. They were known at the time as Mk II(DC) aircraft, but retrospectively came to be called T Mk IIIs.

The Photographic Reconnaissance Unit, Benson, had tested the Mosquito as a lone operator. Neither enemy fighters nor guns had been able to catch a Mosquito until December 1941 when 'Benedictine' (W4055) fell to anti-aircraft gunners near Bergen in Norway. By then the first bombers were in RAF hands.

The squadron chosen to try out the bomber was 105 which had endured harsh action in France in 1940, and since then had been flying Blenheims within 2 Group. It was to the squadron's base at Swanton Morley in Norfolk that Geoffrey de Havilland Jr flew W4064 on November 15 1941. The newcomer was a dashing performer and young Geoffrey threw the aeroplane around in his inimitable manner. The Mosquito needed no Blenheim gunner, so those in 105 Squadron were at once redundant. Some immediately asked to remuster for observer/navigator training, hoping to get back to Mosquitoes. They needed to be very fit, for Bomber Command intended to use the aircraft as a lone high-level operator. Medium-level operations were judged too hazardous for an unarmed bomber, but one of the reasons why a handful of Mosquito bombers had come along before they were ready for operational use was to allow Bomber Command to decide upon their most useful employment.

It was not long before the amazing capabilities of the Mosquito bomber were clear beyond any doubt. W4065 was pitted against AFDU's Spitfires at Duxford — and it out-performed them.

105 Squadron moved to Horsham St Faith near Norwich in December 1941. Vital range estimation flights followed, high-level navigation and special flying training, for the bomber type. Not only could it fly fast to bomb a target, it could just as readily carry a mixture of bombs and cameras — an ideal combination.

Meanwhile the PRU was busily employing its aircraft on long sorties. Ten PR 1s were in use by January 1942, which meant that, because the PR aircraft had been diverted to bomber role reconnaissance, machines became in very short supply. By the end of February 1942 88 PR sorties had been flown and still only one aircraft was missing. Luckily more Mosquito PR aircraft would become available, from a batch of 50 Mosquitoes ordered in April 1941. Now that these were to be completed as bombers a few could be diverted for special PR duties as PR Mk IVs.

January 1942 saw the entry to service of the fighter when one of the 'DC' ex-turret aircraft, W4073, arrived at Castle Camps where newly-formed 157 Squadron was in the process of arriving from the airfield's parent station, Debden. Castle Camps in 11 Group was an awful place for anyone to live. It had been lifted from satellite to full station status, but was still able only to accommodate one squadron. Still surprising, it is, that this station on a hill top, cold and very wet in winter, extremely hot in summer, should have been chosen. But it was reasonably close to Hatfield and at the time quite remotely situated from prying eyes.

About a month after the Mosquitoes had arrived and were often seen displaying their sleek black forms in the

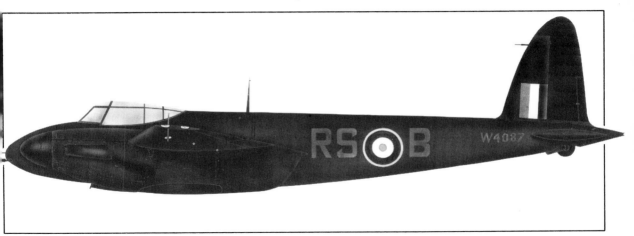

In a rough matt black finish, Mosquito NF II W4087 arrived at 32 MU St Athan for AI radar on February 13 1942. It joined 157 Squadron at Castle Camps on March 9 1942, one of its first Mk IIs. After use for operational training it joined 1422 Flight, Heston, on May 5 1942. Handling trials preceded it getting a nose Turbinlite. It was first flown thus on December 1 1942, proceeded to Wittering on January 7 1943 and there was flown by a 532 Squadron crew before passing to 85 Squadron, Hunsdon, in February 1943. The airborne searchlight was outdated so the aircraft returned to 1422 Flight in August 1943 staying for general radio trials until autumn 1944. Its subsequent research and development use is unknown. It was struck off charge on January 30 1946. It is shown in 157 Squadron's markings.

area, local heads had already been poked into them. They had read a notice in the cockpit — 'not to be dived at over 450 mph'. Someone had raised that figure to a mere 600 mph and within Cambridgeshire the Mosquito was known for sure to be a wonder plane. What was certainly true, and also widely known by now, was that the new shape was a winner, and a very fast one.

The length of the run at Castle Camps was none too great for Mosquitoes. It was March before full night flying training was permitted, and a few weeks later before Mk IIs, fully equipped with AI Mk V radar, reached the squadron. A few detailed modifications were necessary after a period of night flying, by which time the longer-established 151 Squadron based at Wittering had received Mk IIs.

Rivalry to get the machines into action was abounding. 157 Squadron was led by Wing Commander Gordon Slade who after the war became a test pilot for Fairey Aviation. The commanding officer of 151 Squadron was Wing Commander Smith behind whom stood the indomitable figure of Basil Embry, Station Commander at Wittering.

Throughout April 1942 both fighter squadrons and the lone bomber squadron worked up, the former by night and the latter by day. Night machine-gun firing caused such brilliance that the pilot, so close to the guns, was temporarily blinded. Special flash eliminators were required. A more serious problem had yet again reared its head, for the cowling panels by the hefty flare-damping shrouds were again burning through. The exhaust system was troublesome and brought many problems to maintenance crews before it was modified, albeit over a long period. Tailwheel problems were

finally overcome when the unusual twin-tread Marstrand type came into use.

Mosquito NF IIs were entering operational service at a time when enemy night bomber activity on a low scale, comprised mainly of low level mining, took place off the East Coast. That is, until Hitler became enraged by the success of British fire bomb attacks on Lübeck and Rostock. By way of reply he ordered attacks against British historic cities many of which had escaped much bombing since they were of little military or strategic merit. On April 27 1942 Norwich was the target and 157 Squadron was scrambled and sent after the raiders. The enemy needed to spend but a few minutes over East Anglia to attack the city and the Mosquitoes, although responding rapidly, had no success. Further attacks in the 'Baedeker series' brought enemy bombers within both Castle Camps and Wittering areas, but no successes were achieved in April.

The Baedeker raids continued into May, Dornier Do 217s forming the main element of the enemy force. They were quite fast and would fly rather low, and at 300 mph meant a tough quarry for both Mosquito and radar plotter. But on May 29 1942, during a Luftwaffe raid on Grimsby, Flight Lieutenant Pennington of 151 Squadron contacted a raider over the sea. He exchanged fire and the bomber, believed at the time to be a Heinkel He 111 but more likely a Do 217E of KG 2, was claimed. Shortly before dawn on May 30 Squadron Leader Ashfield of 157 Squadron was guided by radar to a Do 217E south of Dover. He pumped his ammunition into the bomber which then dived steeply into cloud. A tracking coastal radar station lost trace of the enemy when he was ten miles south of Dover. It is possible that

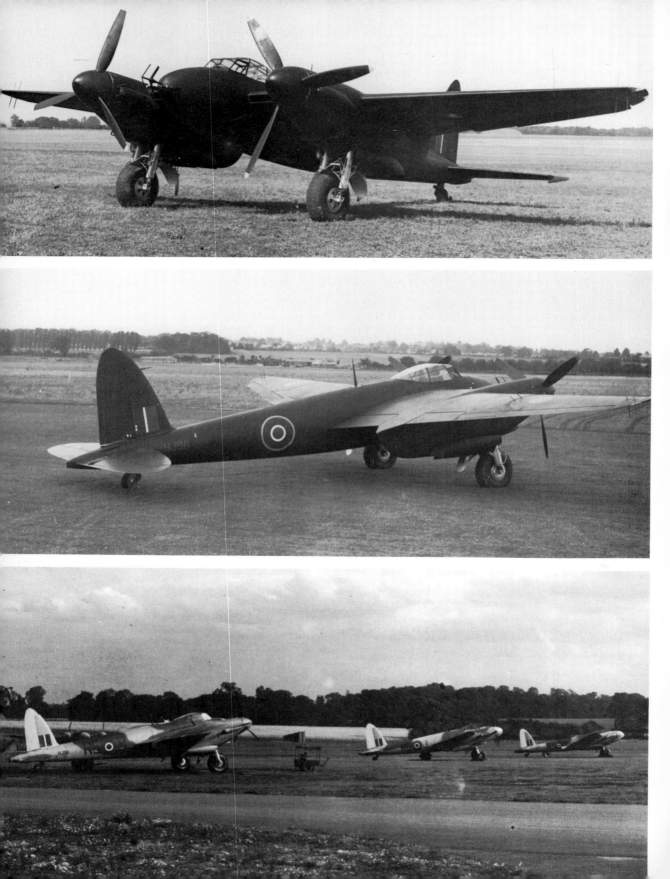

Above left *Airborne Identification radar aerials adorn Mosquito NF II DD737 (serial number Dull Red). Aircraft served with 85 Squadron, 264 Squadron and was lost during service with the Bomber Support Development Unit in December 1944* (de Havilland).

Left *HJ911 was a late production Mk II, Leavesden-built.*

Below left *Mosquito IIs of 157 Squadron dispersed at Hunsdon. HJ911 nearest, now RS:H, wears a very unusual camouflage pattern for a Mosquito. The colour is Dark Green and Medium Sea Grey. DD641 RS:N, far distant, also features an unusual pattern of camouflage. Both aircraft had once been matt black over-all.*

Above *Mosquito II W4087 in rough matt black finish wears the identity letters RS:B of 157 Squadron. Later it became the Turbinlite Mosquito* (Kyle Webster).

Right *Photographed in February 1942, the cannon installation in the Mosquito NF II* (de Havilland).

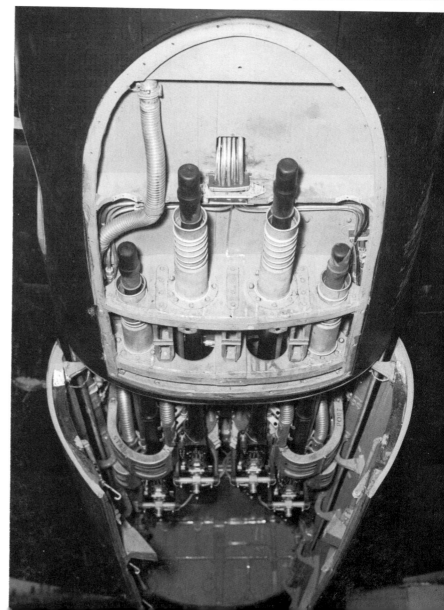

Mosquito B Mk IV srs ii DZ360, wearing Dark Green/Ocean Grey-Medium Sea Grey finish with Sky codes and black serials, served with 105 Squadron from November 6 1942. It was loaned to 139 Squadron for three low-level raids on rail targets, at Hengelo on December 9 1942, Tergnier on December 13 and the Meppen area on December 20. On December 22 1942 after attacking rail sheds at Termonde it was shot down by AA fire near Dunkirk.

this Do 217 came down off the Dutch coast, one of four Do 217s lost during that night's operations. Of 151 Squadron's earlier claims enemy records show no evidence of a loss, although that is no certain reason for discounting the success. It does at least seem very likely that by May 30 a Mosquito had made a kill. A second was imminent.

Bomber Mk IV Mosquitoes were put on to the production line at Hatfield in February 1942. By May there were, however, still only eight Mosquito bombers on 105 Squadron's strength including the first Mk IV srs ii bomber, DK288. The early Mk IV srs i, or B/PRU conversion, was showing a top speed of about 382 mph TAS at 18,000 ft when carrying a full bomb and fuel load.

The small number of bombers available was far too small to employ for any length of time. The Mosquito had now been in service for six months and it was judged that crew morale could easily suffer from this long work-up period. Not before the end of April did short-tailed bombs reach Horsham. Then late in May 1942, 105 Squadron received its first Operations Order since re-equipping. The squadron would use its Mosquitoes to make harrassing attacks throughout the day following the great 1,000 bomber raid on Cologne. Four Mosquito crews would operate, singly, during the day each taking four 500 lb MC bombs to Cologne.

At dawn on May 31 Squadron Leader Oakeshott left in W4072:GB-D to make the first Mosquito bombing sortie, and on reaching Cologne he discovered smoke billowing to 14,000 ft. He was flying much higher and bombs could only be aimed, hopefully, through the smoke.

The second aircraft to go, W4064, met with disaster for it fell to enemy anti-aircraft fire, although the Germans learnt very little from the shattered wreckage — except that that aircraft was made of wood.

Two late morning sorties were despatched, then came the final run of the day, by Squadron Leader Channer. He was to make a low-level PR sortie over the hotly defended city. Cologne was still swathed in smoke, but by going in low Channer unwittingly became a trail blazer. His safe return proved that the Mosquito could penetrate a heavily defended zone relying upon its speed for survival.

So now bomber, fighter and reconnaissance aircraft, all the three major variants of the Mosquito, were fully operational. The prelude had been played, the main opera would follow.

Chapter Three

'Please can we have our chimney back?'

By June 1942 Mosquito reconnaissance aircraft were ranging as far as Marseilles and the Italian naval base at Spetzia, during the month in which they sought the *Tirpitz* in Norwegian waters. That flight involved a round journey of 3,000 miles completed in a day and including a refuelling stop in the USSR. In the context of history this may be seen as a portent for those memorable days in the early 1950s when the Comet jet airliner made equally spectacular day return journeys to distant places in a manner hitherto unknown — just as was the case with the Mosquito in its time.

One of the more unusual twists to the Mosquito story came on August 24 1942 when one of the few PR IVs was despatched to photograph Italian targets, including Venice where use was being made of an area which should not have been subject to attack. DK310's luck ran out when it developed a glycol leak and had to land at Belp in neutral Switzerland. There was considerable concern lest the Germans somehow found out too much about this Mosquito. It was, however, promptly interned and locked away by the Swiss - for the present. The Swiss negotiated with the British until it was agreed that the aircraft could be passed to Swissair to make internal night mail runs, and bear a new identity B-4.

This scheme came to nothing and the machine was returned to the Swiss Air Force. Later it served as a test-bed for the N-20 flying for ten years, during the period 1943-53.

It was clear that two major modifications would make the Mosquito an even more superior aircraft for reconnaissance operations, and the spin-off into other roles would be equally worthwhile. Both concerned high-altitude performance. If the Mosquito could maintain superior performance over enemy fighters then such immunity obviously increased its viability.

The first modification along these lines concerned the fitting of two-stage Merlin engines, for which purpose the mainplanes of W4050 returned to Salisbury Hall in October 1941. The new Merlin 61 engines arrived there in February 1942 and carried W4050 aloft for the first time in June, conferring greater speed and a higher ceiling.

This improvement was of little avail operationally unless the crew could travel in reasonable comfort, and that meant cabin pressurisation. A special airframe, MP469, was set aside for such a feature and, fitted with Merlin 61s, this aircraft also flew in June 1942. In the month following, W4050 reached a speed of 432 mph,

Late in its active life, W4050 is seen with Merlin two-stage engines and the usual Dark Green, Dark Earth, Yellow finish and yellow prototype marking. Serial was also yellow at this stage (photographed in 1944).

and the new engines were able to lift the aircraft to 40,000 ft. The first application of these engines was in the PR Mk IV DK324 which then became the PR VIII. Mosquitoes for lower-level operations were not being neglected though, as plans went ahead for the B and PR Mk Vs and the NF/FB/LRF Mk VI based upon the Mk II but carrying extra fuel and bombs on wing racks. And, whilst development plans went ahead at Hatfield, much was happening to the Mosquitoes already in service.

The third fighter squadron to equip was 264 Squadron at Colerne where Mosquitoes arrived in May 1942. They were entering service when Luftwaffe night bomber activity against Britain was again slowing down. There was little action for any night fighter Mosquitoes until late June 1942, by the end of which period 151 Squadron has claimed four enemy aircraft. In July it claimed five. To 157 Squadron it seemed that their competitors had all the good fortune. Enemy aircraft persistently operated either to the north or south of 157's operations area, or alternatively they were flying very low-level mining sorties. No 85 Squadron was now receiving Mosquitoes, 151's score seemed to be steadily rising and 157 were left on the sidelines after their pioneering effort.

There was little night trade in August 1942 but 157's luck changed on August 22. Wing Commander Slade shot down a Do 217E of II/KG2, the wreckage of which was clear for all to see near Worlingworth, close to Mildenhall in Suffolk.

Before the end of 1942 four more night fighter squadrons had equipped wtith Mosquitoes, Squadrons 25, 307, 410 and 456, but there had been problems with water seepage and thus a need for some waterproofing.

One thing had become very clear. The Mosquito was a fast aircraft to employ against relatively slow night bombers. Practised techniques were essential. There were cases of Mosquitoes overshooting Ju 88s and Do 217s, as a result of which some strange looking, frill-like Youngman airbrakes were fitted, encircling the mid-fuselage of W4052. Various widths of brake vanes were tried, but by then it was techniques in operational situations which solved the difficulties. It was clear, too, that the Mosquito might be better off with even higher speed at low levels as well as at far greater altitudes, especially if enemy night raiders flew faster in future. The thick matt black finish of the NF IIs was found to reduce their top speed from 378 mph to 352 mph TAS. It also revealed the fighter's fine silhouette on all but the darkest nights. In September 1942 steps came about whereby the Dark Green/Medium Sea Grey finish common to so many Mosquitoes was introduced and the all-black scheme very rapidly passed from view.

Already there were many RAF claimants for the Mosquito. Indeed, every Command had thought up good reasons for using them — except for Bomber Command. Within that organisation there remained uncertainty as to what use the light bomber could be. Wedded to a sledgehammer war the Command had yet to appreciate the important part the Mosquito bomber would come to play.

A small group within Fighter Command who appreciated its potential called themselves 23 Squadron, and they were based at Ford. Since the end of 1940 they had waged a very useful campaign at night by intruding upon enemy bomber bases in occupied territory. Their success was not only to be measured by the number of German aircraft they shot down, one would also have to look at their nuisance value in interrupting operations.

During 1941-2 23 Squadron switched from using antique Blenheim 1s to an assortment of Douglas Boston intruders. The Boston in a low-level bombing role was good, and its story has a parallel with that of the Mosquito bomber since only Fighter Command could find a role for it as a heavily armed night fighter or as an intruder. Those examples with 23 Squadron were virtually bombers, for it was not practicable to operate them in a fighter-bomber role. In any case the Boston's range was insufficient, whereas when 23 Squadron heard about the Mosquito it seemed to them the ideal answer for their needs. The famed Squadron Leader 'Sammy' Hoare made enquiries at Hatfield in April 1942 and set the idea forth for a Mosquito intruder, a fighter-bomber. It was well worth a try and, when Fighter Command was approached, they approved the idea for

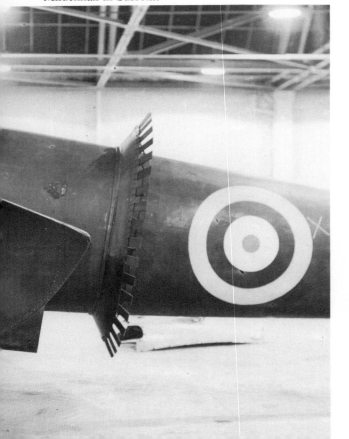

The Youngman frill airbrake was one attempt to slow the early night fighter as it lined up on its quarry (de Havilland).

25 Mosquito IIs to be fitted out as intruders. These, taken from the fighter batch, came available quickly because they needed no AI radar. Bombs would not be carried, but 23 Squadron did not worry for eight guns were good enough for any fighter. Mosquito DZ434 was quickly taken from the lines too, had a bomb-bay fitted aft of the cannon and as HJ662, the prototype fighter-bomber Mk VI, flew in June 1942.

Very soon after 23 Squadron began to equip with Mosquitoes designated Mk II (Special Intruder). Operations commenced in July and on merely the second night of operations, with only one Mosquito available, 'Sammy' Hoare shot down a Do 217 at Montdidier. Two nights later an He 111 and Do 217 fell to the same aircraft and by July 31 DD670:YP-S had four enemy aircraft to its credit making it easily the current top scorer.

The scheme to make the Mosquito an intruder was to prove as important a development line as any, for it was but a small step to carrying bombs and thereby producing a superlative fighter-bomber which, by November 1942, could be seen to have an operational and fully-loaded range of 1,200 miles.

Meanwhile, 23 Squadron operated busily and effectively for the rest of 1942, from Ford and later Manston and Bradwell Bay. Then, close to Christmas 1942, the squadron was ordered to use its talent in the Mediterranean Theatre, and at a time when the Mosquito bomber was also about to prove of exceptional value to Bomber Command.

Before that event, much was to happen to the small Mosquito day bomber force in 2 Group. In May 1942, the month when the bomber first saw action, a Mk IV,DK290, which was to figure in many Mosquito bomber trials, was found able to carry four 500 lb bombs in its belly, double the load originally envisaged. In the manner planned for the first true bomber, the Mk V, it could also carry a 250 lb bomb beneath each mainplane. A sizeable load indeed for a small aeroplane.

Whilst this important programme was being worked out the handful of bomber Mosquitoes with 105 Squadron were being used as lone high-altitude nuisance daylight raiders in a manner which, in later years, would again be out of all proportion to their cost in machines and men.

A second bomber squadron, 139, began to form on June 8 1942 but because aircraft were in such short supply their crews had to use 105's aircraft whenever they operated, a situation unaltered until December 1942. In June the bombers were first operated at night, attacking airfields during the 1,000 bomber raid on Bremen. Thus, they had become round-the-clock bombers, the only aircraft really to attain that distinction.

Mosquitoes of 105 Squadron prepare for a typical group take-off from Marham (Flight International).

A turning point in the Mosquito's career, though seen as such only in retrospect, was Squadron Leader Channer's low-level raid on the first day of operations. Low-level daylight bombing had much to commend it, always assuming the bomber returned safely. Therefore, on July 2 1942, six Mosquitoes set off for a low-level attack on a maritime target at Flensburg. There remains little doubt that they should have all returned for, in the situation in which they found themselves, it was proven that they could draw away even from the new Fw 190. But Bomber Command had yet to realise the importance of carefully devising the routing of bombing raids. On this occasion the Mosquitoes were tracked very effectively by enemy radar, and this cost two aircraft and crews.

Nine days later they were again directed to Flensburg, this time providing a diversion for the Lancaster raid on Danzig. Again, they flew low over the sea, thus making detection difficult. Additionally, the route taken was far safer for them — unless they flew too low over a smooth sea or, like Sergeant Rowlands, brought back a very visible souvenir from Denmark. So low did he fly that he clipped a chunk of chimney pot from a house. It crashed into the cockpit and was brought home as a trophy which still testifies to Rowlands' low flying. What the Dane who lost his chimney pot said seems never to have been recorded . . .

Largely immune as it was to enemy interception, the Mosquito was nevertheless far from a safe ride. Indeed, the loss rate on some early raids was as high as 16 per cent, but then such loss rates were commonplace in 2 Group for the first two years of the war. The crews were sure that they could work out suitable techniques to reduce the Mosquito losses which were not attributable to the aircraft's performance but due to the manner of operation. Weather was a determining factor and routing and times of attack were clearly worth considering.

By July, with effective action to its credit, the Mosquito was held in high regard by maintenance crews since repair was indeed simple. A saw, a pot of glue, the right piece of wood and a steady hand could work wonders. Interchangeability of components was good, especially so when one considers that the furniture makers had to learn to work with great accuracy. Little wonder, then, that there were more and more demands for Mosquitoes.

Proof of the ability of the Mosquito to outpace the Fw 190, the latest German fighter, came when one of these aircraft landed in error at Pembrey in South Wales. Flight trials showed that the Mosquito was faster at all likely operating altitudes — but only by a few miles per hour. Operational techniques could do a lot to improve that small gap.

Prime German targets sooner or later had to come along for the aircraft. 2 Group had laid various plans to attack Berlin when 90 Squadron was flying Fortress 1s in 1941. Bad weather, contrailing and the certain risk of detection — and worse — caused them all to be abandoned. Berlin, and bombing in daylight — this was surely the best thing Bomber Command could achieve with the war going none too well.

There was little doubt that the Mosquito could reach Berlin, it had been proven during range estimation trials. But 'ampg' tests are one thing, and only a trial operation could really prove if Mosquitoes could attack Berlin in daylight, or night time. It would be no mean achievement.

The date chosen for the raid was September 19 1942, and six crews set off from Horsham St Faith on the long journey. They were to use a Lo-Hi-Lo flight profile, flying independently for safety. The small number involved seemed likely to make them easily detected. There was, however, cloud cover, but this in turn made target identification very difficult. Only one crew claimed to bomb the city. One of the others was shot down during a raid which seemed like a fiasco —

Below far left *KB161 'VANCOUVER' was, in the hands of 139 Squadron, the first Canadian-built Mosquito to fly an operational sortie. The Sky spinners and band were removed before this event.*

Below left *The Canadian-built equivalent of the British FB Mk VI was the FB Mk 26 an example of which, KA131, is seen here. The main difference lay in the Packard Merlin engines.*

Right *KA888, one of the few Mosquito T 27s built. The T Mk 22 was the Canadian equivalent of the British T Mk III. With Packard Merlin 225s the T 27 was its successor (David Menard).*

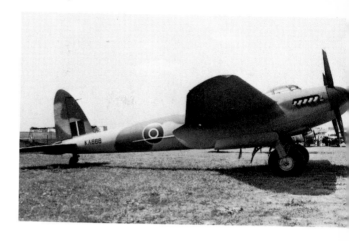

although one which provided proof that Mosquitoes could bomb Berlin and probably return from even such a distant target, and in daylight if the raid planning was good.

Another September event was equally important. Canada, where de Havilland had a branch, was clearly a safe place for aircraft production. Little wonder, then, that de Havilland (Canada) were now building Mosquito bombers and it was one of these, KB300 a Mk VII, which made its maiden flight on September 24. Four Canadian examples were flying by the end of December 1942 and a sample Mk II DD664 had reached the Australian subsidiary.

If September 24 1942 was an important date, then surely the morrow was to rank even higher. It marked the 22nd birthday of the de Havilland enterprise and 105 Squadron, as elite now as the makers, decided to give the company a special present whilst also presenting one to the enemy. 2 Group chose as their target the Gestapo HQ in Oslo. Bombing a precision target, the dream of 2 Group at all times, was always difficult and when it lay amongst one's Allies it was a task not readily to be undertaken. But there was general feeling that the excellence of the Mosquito's qualities was such that low-level precision attacks could be carried out.

Squadron Leader George Parry led the four aircraft which set out from Leuchars and approached Oslo along its fjord. Fighters had been alerted and one Mosquito hit by cannon and machine-gun fire came down. Bombs from the Mosquitoes mostly fell around the building, some passing through, but the success of the raid was not only to be measured in bombing accuracy. The Mosquitoes raced away from the city clocking up 330 mph IAS as they drew away from the pursuing fighters. Back at Sumburgh, where they landed, there was immediate discussion of a vital aspect of the flight — the possible range of the aircraft. It seemed feasible that with a carefully chosen flight profile the bomber could fly 1,300 miles fully laden, but it was finally decided that 1,220 miles was a more realistic figure.

One thing was now certain, the Mosquito unarmed

could attack distantly — and survive. It was still uncertain whether the enemy knew the Mosquito bombers were unarmed. There was some unease about the absence of guns and the RAF put forward the idea of a scare gun, or two, placed in the nacelles or somewhere on the rear fuselage. Their weight penalty might have been crucial to survival, and a cable-operated gun would soon be discovered as a pointless ruse. A hand-held gun poked from the canopy was another possibility, but it came to nothing. What was instead done was to paint some of the Mosquito bombers to look like RAF fighters by adding Sky bands and spinners, but even this was short-lived. Low-level camouflage proved a safer scheme.

Clearly, an increase in speed was desirable, bearing in mind the minimal advantage held over the Fw 190 — perhaps, in the worst case, a mere 5 mph. Stub exhausts would be an advance over the bulky saxophone flame dampers which were of no value on a day bomber. It was therefore decided to mix the aircraft so that some retained dampers for possible night flying. Much attention was given to details such as replacing the aerial mast by a whip aerial.

In hilly terrain, where low-level, contour-hugging attacks were too hazardous, the tactic now was to employ a shallow dive. This was developed and, in conjunction with low-level attack, formed a very useful style of operation which was often practised. The low-level force would race in — and low-level really did mean *low* flying — whilst the shallow dive force would climb shortly before the target then dive into the attack thus much confusing enemy gunners. Both groups would then indulge in a low-level escape. The enemy coast would usually be crossed fast and low, but there was the ever present risk of bird strike, to which there was no real answer. Leading ornithologists were asked to submit details of areas of the European coastline where birds could be expected in large numbers. Quite a number of operations were mounted at dawn or dusk, again bringing bird strike problems, although using some cover of darkness was valuable.

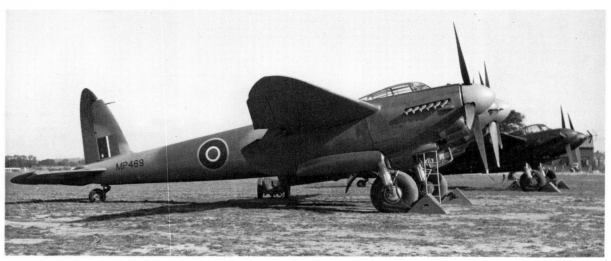

Above *MP469 was transformed from a high flying bomber into a high flying fighter in less than a week, in an attempt to defeat the Ju 86 high flying bomber. The Grey-Green camouflage was supplemented by deep blue under surfaces* (de Havilland).

Below *The flight line at Hatfield on November 2 1942. Bombers DZ372, DZ371 and DZ362 stand out on account of their darker grey camouflage. The Grey-Green Mk IIs are DZ253 and DZ255. DZ372:GB-C crashed in March 1943, DZ371 was lost on her only sortie directed against Philips of Eindhoven. DZ362 was used by 521 (Met) Squadron.*

This famous Mosquito, LR507, completed 148 operational sorties almost immune from damage and during nearly two years of sustained operations. A B Mk IX, it joined 109 Squadron at Marham on June 17 1943 then on July 5 passed to 105 Squadron. Initial operations consisted of route and Oboe marking of Ruhr and Rhineland targets. On July 13 1943 LR507 attempted 105 Squadron's first Mosquito IX marking operation, against Cologne. It was taken to Bourn on March 23 1944 when the squadron moved there to begin intensive operations. The night of the Normandy invasion was when LR507, marked Maisy, started a hectic few days, for the next night Chateaudun was marked, next night Versailles marshalling yard and next night Mayenne. On the evening of June 19 its markers fell on Watten V-site and, naturally, LR507 marked many oil targets. It also marked for the massive day raids to enable the army to break out from Caen and, in July 1944, flew 15 sorties. It helped to reduce Calais in September 1944 and was used on April 9 1945 to make the first Oboe-led raid on Berlin. Cheated of success, it returned two nights later — successfully. And how could LR507 do otherwise than help lead the Bomber Command attack on Berchtesgaden, Hitler's alpine retreat, at the end of the war? A remarkable aeroplane which, after reaching 22 MU on September 21 1945, was struck off charge on May 15 1946 and sadly broken up. Its finish rarely changed and here it is shown in Ocean Grey—Dark Green—Medium Sea Grey with red codes and black serials as recorded in April 1944 at Bourn.

High-level bombing raids had all but been abandoned by September 1942. Contrails made it easy for a fighter to 'jump' a lone Mosquito, but this was a risk PR crews had to take and try in the process to avoid contrail heights. There were still too few bombers to make much impact, due of course to official policies. The contrast between stereotyped official outlook and the enterprise for which the great name of de Havilland for ever stood was no better shown that at the start of September 1942.

A conference took place at Hatfield when, at midday, there came an uninvited interruption. In recent weeks the Luftwaffe on fine days had operated over Britain some very high-flying Ju 86s fitted with pressure cabins and carrying small loads. They flew very slowly, but at heights where they were virtually immune for even the high-flying Spitfires were unable to reach them. One of the raiders had the temerity to fly over Hatfield on its way to bomb Luton. On seeing the sauce of the raider de Havilland replied almost without much consideration that they could produce a Mosquito to catch an intruder — and within a week. The MAP representatives at Hatfield could barely believe that, although de Havilland had surprised such people so many times. Could everything be possible at Hatfield?

Indeed it seemed so. That pressure cabin high flier prototype MP469 existed as a bomber. A quick cut with a saw, here and there, and the nose was off and a new

one fitted carrying guns. And, just one week after, the bomber-cum-fighter was clambering to 40,000 ft and more. Next day it was positioned at Northolt to provide a fine welcome for the next Ju 86. None came, but the high-altitude conversion was not so easily neglected and in 1943 a handful of similar Mk XVs with AI radar were built and used by 85 Squadron who had them in hand in case specialised high raiders came again. The high flier programme convinced the company of the need for a pressure cabin in such aircraft, cavity windows to prevent condensation, a wing span of about 60 ft, possibly four-bladed propellers and, of course, two-stage Merlin engines. Merlin 76/77s were tested in W4050 in October 1942 and these brought the very high speeds already mentioned.

By November 1942 the enthusiasm for the Mosquito bomber, among both squadrons now at Marham, was tremendous and they were making themselves into a small, efficient and highly elitist force the like of which was always far from generally popular in Bomber Command, committed as it was to large numbers of slow, heavily armed bombers which were costly, like their aircrew training programmes. There was, too, the obsession now with night attack. This was a false liking forced upon the Command because of its inability to mount heavy successful daylight raids.

It was, however, in the late summer of 1942, that the

Mosquito's place in Bomber Command became assured. The value of a special pathfinding force to mark and lead night attacks, whilst being unpopular with many in the Command, remained really unassailable. Certainly there remained valid arguments against such an idea, but from a cost-effective viewpoint, and certainly an operational one, to have specially trained marker crews was a sensible idea. At this time a new radio aid, Oboe, was sufficiently developed for operational trials. It might have been carried in the high-flying Wellington Mk VI, but this was a slow aeroplace which had produced many problems. Instead, a handful of Mosquitoes were delivered first to Stradishall then Wyton for 109 Squadron, which was already famous for its radio warfare work.

By flying along a beam directed at a target the aircraft could be held on a very accurate course. Then upon receiving a different signal from another station beamed across the aircraft's track, the target's position was signalled and bombs could be dropped. But it was not primarily bombs which 109 Squadron would use. Instead, it would first be flares and, in later months, target indicators. Much to 139 Squadron's disgust 109 Squadron had received their allocation of Mosquitoes. Before 109 Squadron tried out Oboe blind bombing, though, 139 Squadron had been equipped with their own aircraft — at last — and flew them on the famous low-level 2 Group raid on the Phillips' works at Eindhoven on December 6 1942. Proving ubiquity on that occasion, a Mosquito reconnoitred the route to be flown by the large force, then another Mosquito photographed the result of the attacks.

On December 20 1942 109 Squadron tried out Oboe, taking as their target the power station at Lutterade in Holland. Four of the six aircraft despatched dropped markers followed by 500 lb MC bombs delivered from 26,000 ft. The higher the aircraft flew, the greater the range of Oboe, which was established as 275 miles at 28,000 ft; which meant that its range was limited to the Ruhr and parts of north-west Germany. Such high flying was beyond any other Allied bomber then operating, only the Mosquito could serve in the new role. It was indeed a hazardous one for the course had to be held for the last ten minutes of the target run in — which meant that with one pair of stations operating only one aircraft could be handled in ten minutes. It was very essential that the marking be accurate. In December 1942 sky markers were tried for the first time during a raid on Düsseldorf. Ground markers were first used in January 1943 during which month 109 Squadron flew 15 nights of operations.

It was not to be long before, at last, Bomber Command rapidly warmed to the Mosquito idea. If the aircraft could mark very accurately for the main force, then it should equally be able to indulge in very accurate bombing of quite small targets even at night.

Thus, by the end of 1942, the role of the Mosquito had multiplied far beyond expectations. Reconnaissance aircraft, day and night fighter, fighter-intruder, round-the-clock bomber, and now the unwanted had become the prized. And the Mosquito was soon to become the very spearhead of the bomber offensive.

Chapter Four

A hectic life

By January 1943 600 firms were involved in building, or helping to build, Mosquitoes. They ranged from small groups of elderly people working in garages — or even garden sheds — to great concerns now geared to fast production methods. The number of Mosquito variants was growing rapidly and in January 1943 the first Mk II fighter arrived at Marshall of Cambridge to have its machine-guns swopped for centimetric AI Mk VIII radar fitted within a thimble-shaped radome which accommodated a scanner. Marshall worked very fast and in March 85 Squadron took delivery of the first F Mk XII conversion from the Mk II. Mk VIII AI was to prove a great advance over the old 'bow and arrow' Mk V.

Almost at the same time work was commenced on the 'bull nosed' or Universal nose radome primarily to accommodate American SCR720 radar which, when wedded to the strong-wing FB VI airframe, resulted in the Mosquito NF XIII. This could have either the 'thimble nose' or the 'bull nose' radome. Using the fighter-bomber wing meant that it was possible for this new variant to carry wing drop tanks and, very rarely, bombs.

In January 1943 eight night fighter squadrons had Mosquito IIs, but there was little enemy night activity over Britain and what did take place was mainly directed against London. Night defence of the capital was particularly conducted by 85 Squadron commanded by the most famous night fighter pilot of all, Wing Commander John Cunningham. It was to his squadron that the first Mk XIIs went and the first kill with the new version came on April 14/15 during a raid on Chelmsford.

One of the main lines of development now was to fit Merlin 25 engines which boosted the aircraft's low-level performance. These engines were installed in many Mk VIs which at the start of 1943 were beginning to be built. At the other end of the scale two-stage Merlin engines were being installed in a handful of Mk IVs which, converted to the PR role, became Mk VIIIs with a top speed of about 420 mph. Despite their small number they proved very useful until the fully-modified Mk IX airframe for the Merlin 61 series became available.

Already the Mosquito was being employed in one totally unexpected fashion, one which must have brought special pleasure to Sir Geoffrey de Havilland, for he never disguised his desire for the company to be in the forefront of airliner design. British Overseas Airways Corporation had, for much of the war, maintained a mail and passenger service to neutral Sweden. They were using a few Douglas DC-3s for this run and desired faster aircraft. Late in 1942 interest swung to the possibility of using Mosquitoes as special mail carriers. A radical suggestion, that of converting the bomb bay to accommodate passengers, albeit in utmost discomfort, was but a pace away. Flying high, in cold conditions and wearing an oxygen mask for much of the journey must have been an unforgettable experience. Yet it was a flight made by many whose names are universally

The long-span wings of the Mosquito Mk XV night fighter are very obvious here, along with its black nose radome and the additional air intakes below the mainplane.

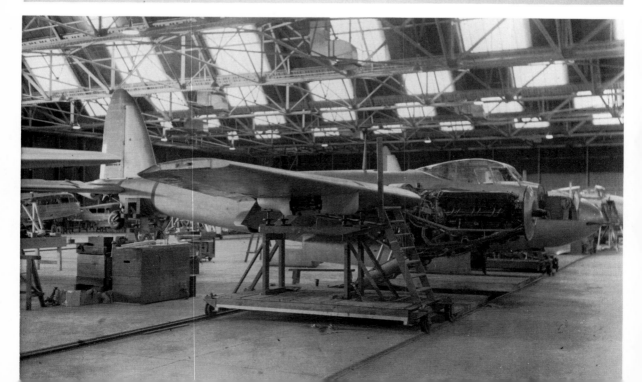

Above left *This Mosquito NF XIII features the 'thimble'-shaped radome as fitted to the Mk XII and Mk XVII also. Later Mk XIIIs had a Universal Nose Radome. HK425 here is coded K:RO and served with 29 Squadron from January to October 1944* (de Havilland).

Left *The lines of the 'thimble' nose were none too clean, otherwise the Mosquito XIII seen here surely looks beautiful* (de Havilland).

Below left *The airframe DZ434 became HJ662. Seen under construction here, it served as the prototype Mk VI fighter-bomber* (de Havilland).

Above *Mk VI HJ719 photographed in May 1943 has yet to acquire bomb rack fairings. Finish is as for the night fighters, Medium Sea Grey with disruptive Dark Green on upper surfaces. A few such Mosquitoes had darker grey on their upper surfaces. Note the five-stack exhausts* (de Havilland).

Below *As it peels away a Mk VI fighter-bomber reveals its wing bomb racks, belly bays and a useful amount of detail for any modeller* (de Havilland).

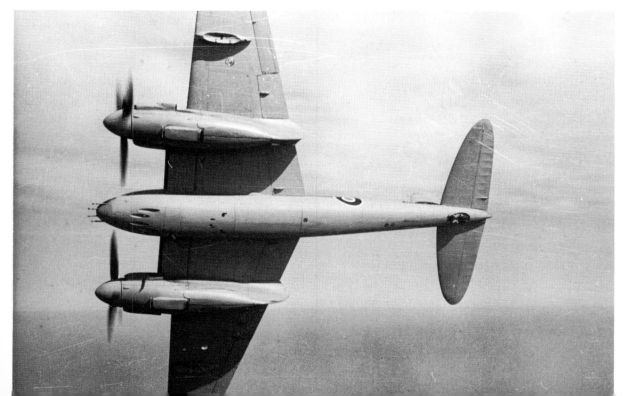

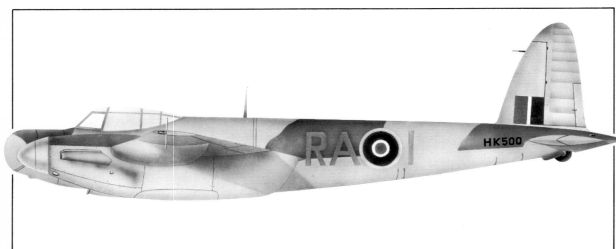

known. Careful routing between Leuchars and Bromma was needed. The service, which commenced on February 4 1943, continued until May 1945, first with Mk IVs and later unarmed Mk VIs.

As pilots of the BOAC unit worked up for the commencement of the service another role had come about for the night fighter squadrons. Deprived of action because so few enemy aircraft ventured to Britain, some of the Mosquito IIs had their AI radar removed, then modifications were carried out to permit them to carry long-range wing tanks. Thus equipped, they could indulge in a variety of pernicious operations by day and night over mainland Europe. They could range far, by night and on cloudy days when they could dip below cloud level to attack a wide variety of targets, if opportunity permitted.

At the end of 1942 Mosquitoes had begun to fly patrols over the Bay of Biscay looking for long-range enemy aircraft and also Ju 88C fighters which were trying to interfere with Coastal Command patrols engaged upon locating and attacking U-Boats operating out of the ports of western France. Such Instep patrols were continued to the summer of 1943.

The PR Mk VIII made its first operational sortie on February 19 1943, and then March witnessed the first flight of the production form of the aforementioned type, this being the Mosquito Mk IX. In its bomber version it could carry four 500 lb bombs internally and a 500-pounder beneath each mainplane. The two-stage Merlin engines made it possible for the take-off weight to be as high as 23,000 lb, no small rise. A few weeks later the first examples of the PR Mk IX emerged from the works. This version had a top speed at full load of around 424 mph TAS at 25,000 ft. Thus it was only slightly slower than the then new Mustang when Merlin-engined — whose top speed was 430 mph at 22,000 ft — and faster than the P-47 Thunderbolt which attained 416 mph at 25,000 ft. Thus, now becoming available were variants with improved high- and low-level capabilities. Now the next step would be the ability to lift a load commensurate with the increased engine power available.

Trials with the aircraft in very heavily loaded state had been undertaken by a Farnborough team in August-September 1942 from the airfield known as Blackbushe. They showed that the Mosquito structure could bear an all-up weight of over 25,000 lb. In April 1943 the idea of adapting the Mosquito's bomb bay to carry one 4,000 lb 'cookie' was conceived. The length and girth of the weapon fitted the existing bomb cell, but it required dished doors fully to enclose the weapon, which modification was quite straightforward. It was decided to up-date some Mk IVs to carry the large bomb rather than delay the new two-stage Merlin machines.

Large numbers of the latter would be produced leaving only most fighters and trainers with single-stage engines and they would be produced, initially at any rate, roughly in the proportion of one bomber to five PR aircraft. The reason for this was that for very long daylight sorties these newer engines improved the level of immunity which PR crews needed on their lonely flights to distant Pilsen, Prague and at this time to Peenemünde where the Germans were developing the V1 and V2 weapons. Ranges for such flights were attained with the aid of drop tanks.

Eventually 90 PR IXs were built and powered by Merlin 72/73 engines, left- and right-handed to reduce torque. Early PR Mk Is, now relieved, were used for training and the variety of PR IVs for the development

Above left *Mosquito NF XIII MM446 has a 'thimble' nose and a variety of features applicable to night fighters. The finish is Dark Green and Medium Sea Grey with slightly shiny Night under surfaces. Code letters are Dull Red, serial black. MM446 was delivered to 27 MU on January 30 1944 then to 151 Squadron at Colerne on February 22 1944. This squadron was then engaged upon Insteps and Rangers. During a Day Ranger on May 4 1944 Wing Commander Goodman destroyed four HE 111s at Dijon in MM446. Normandy beach-head patrols were flown, Rangers continued. MM446 had Merlin 25s and because of their superior performance over similar Merlins, this aircraft was one swopped with older Mosquitoes of 96 Squadron when the latter, based at Ford, began night operations against V-1s. MM446 joined 96 Squadron on August 11 1944. On September 24 the squadron moved to Odiham continuing anti-diver patrols. It disbanded on December 12 1944 and MM446 joined 29 Squadron at West Malling for bomber support duties. It was then that the black was applied to the under surfaces. It passed to Marshall's, Cambridge, on February 23 1945 when its squadron re-equipped with Mosquito XXXs. It was drawn at Cambridge on February 25 1945 before being broken up in June 1945.*

Centre left *HK500, a Mk XIII, was fitted with the Universal Nose. In Dark Green and Medium Sea Grey finish with black serials it went to 218 MU on December 20 1943 then joined 410 Night Fighter Squadron at Castle Camps on January 7 1944 becoming RA:I (Dull Red letters). The squadron took HK500 to Hunsdon on April 29 1944, to continue defensive night operations. A move to Zeals came on June 18. Night patrols over the Normandy beach-head were now flown and on June 24 a Ju 188 fell to HK500, 15 miles off Normandy. HK500 was destroyed on July 10 1944 by fire after overshooting Zeals as a result of engine failure. The aircraft is seen as recorded at Castle Camps on April 14 1944.*

Left *Mosquito PR IX LR424 in over-all PR Blue finish. LR424 reached 27 MU on July 22 1943 and joined 540 Squadron at Benson on September 7 1943. It participated in memorable deep penetration reconnaissance flights. Its first attempt to photograph Berlin came on September 25 1943 when Squadron Leader John Merifield found the city cloud clad and noted vapour trails rising from Peenemünde. Damage assessment flights to Berlin came in December and on December 17 1943 LR424's photographs revealed the latest state of things at Peenemünde — with excellent coverage of Berlin, for good measure. Peenemünde fell again to LR424 on December 20 1943 and further vapour trails were noted ascending. On February 9 1944, at the height of the Battle of Berlin, LR424 photographed the city from 33,000 ft — pursued by flak bursts. On February 19 1944, in a similar position, the flak was so intense the aircraft had to leave the city with engines giving full boost. During March 1944 540 Squadron concentrated on targets in southern Europe. On April 10 1944 LR424 failed to return from photographing Friedrichshafen.*

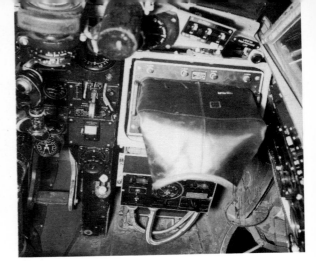

of night photography. A B IV was used for a very new concept in which, by March 1943, it seemed that the Mosquito would have a share.

Through the book and then the film, all the nation has come to know about the fascinating idea of the late Sir Barnes Wallis for a bouncing bomb. Had the full scheme gone through in May 1943, then soon after the German dams were breached Mosquitoes would have homed in on Sumburgh after having sunk the battleship *Tirpitz*.

Development trials of a small, spherical weapon proceeded fast in 1943, but repeated breakages of the casing during impact with the water made it impossible to proceed with the planned attack. There were, and still are, suggestions that the Dams raid seemed much more to official liking than any attack on the *Tirpitz*. Developed at the same time as the bomb designed to breach the dams, the Mosquito weapon had to be very rapidly devised because there was initial reluctance to commission two such devices. This brought a critical situation. The dams could only be breached to best effect when the annual flood water was at its peak. Trials with Highball, the Mosquito weapon, fell into second place — so much so that 617 Squadron's Lancasters alone took the praise, leaving their sister 618 Squadron in the shade. The Mosquito weapon was not ready in time.

For the Mosquito to have dropped the bouncing mines in daylight would have revealed to the foe a very useful technique for anti-shipping operations. When the idea continued to be pursued first for the Pacific war, and then post-war, it remained shrouded in secrecy lest any unfriendly power produced its own bouncing weapons. It remains little known that the post-war variant named Card allowed for two or even four of the weapons to be placed in a crate which could easily be attached to the belly of a variety of aircraft types, in particular to the Sea Hornet making that small, fast fighter a most formidable attack aircraft.

The diversity of Mosquito operations, not to mention Mark numbers, was becoming quite amazing. In April 1943 618 Squadron had formed to use Highball, the 4,000 lb bomb carriage gear was devised and the first fighter-bomber Mk VIs had entered service with 418 Squadron. 256 Squadron was equipping with Mk XIIs (with their centimetric radar), 109 Squadron was receiving its first Mk IXs fitted with Oboe — and, as if this was not enough, there came the truly amazing notion of fitting a six-pounder anti-tank gun into the Mosquito.

Plans to arm it with a mighty gun were nothing new, already a 3.7 in anti-aircraft gun had been suggested. But now a scheme would go ahead with this large anti-tank gun whose prime target would be U-Boats entering

Above left *Cockpit layout of an early Mk VI, photographed in January 1943. The blanked off position to the right would feature a radarscope in a fighter variant* (de Havilland).

Above *The radar operator's equipment tightly fitted into a Mosquito night fighter* (de Havilland).

Left *The swollen bomb-bay on DZ594, the prototype conversion to carry a 4,000 lb 'cookie'.*

Above right *HJ732/G can be seen to have the Molins 57 mm gun poking from its nose, a feature of the FB Mk XVIII. Finish for these aircraft was as for the night fighters* (de Havilland).

Right *Mosquito B Mk IX LR495, the first of the type, was able to carry increased load which could include a 500 lb bomb beneath each wing. It crashed when taking off overloaded on January 29 1944* (de Havilland).

or leaving Biscay ports.

Very quickly after the decision to go ahead with this, the Mk XVIII, the heavy gun arrived at Hatfield. With the 57mm gun installed and firing at the Hatfield butts it showed by its recoil action just how mighty a weapon it was. It was first taken aloft in a Mosquito in June 1943 and entered action in October of that year.

The ultimate major line of Mosquito bomber development also commenced in April 1943. The aircraft could carry a heavy load, it had speed and manoeuvreability — but what it still required was an improvement in high-altitude capability. The engines could take the machine high, but the crew would experience much discomfort. The aircraft needed that pressure cabin. What would instead have to be fitted would be a relatively low-level 2 lb/sq in system which meant that cockpit conditions equated the outside conditions at about 6,000 ft, and the crew continued wearing oxygen masks. Although this was a relatively primitive pressure cabin it did afford more crew comfort, especially on long flights; and for that reason it was yet again the PR version which was first to benefit. The pressurisation system was first fitted to a special prototype, DZ540, which led to the Mk XVI which first flew in July 1943 and was to be able to operate at 40,000 ft.

The value of a high-flying Mosquito was already very apparent to Bomber Command when the Battle of the Ruhr was launched in March 1943. The higher the Oboe force could fly, the longer the effective range of Oboe, although over the Ruhr Mosquitoes were flying so high that wind speeds could much effect accurate marking. Nevertheless, the refined B IXs, and later Mk XVIs, would often find themselves leading the whole of Bomber Command into action, at the head of the Command which had for so long found no particular use for an unarmed bomber.

On the night of March 3/4 1943 the target chosen to open the new bombing phase was the giant Krupp steel works in Essen, hitherto almost entirely unscarred by many RAF attacks. Now it was different for, with Oboe, it was possible to mark a relatively small area, accurately and in darkness so that by dawn the huge armament production centre had been greatly savaged.

May 1943 also witnessed turning points in the Mosquito story. The delivery of the Mk II fighter ended, although it was to continue to operate for some time to come. The wedding of American radar to the Mk II produced the Mk XVII which would play an important part in home defence until the summer of 1944.

In May 1943 both 29 and 256 Squadrons flying Mk XIIs had recorded notable successes in recent weeks. On April 16/17 the Luftwaffe's SKG 10 had commenced using single-seat Fw 190s for night nuisance raids over south-east England and the London area. In some

Above *An alternate wing loading for the two-stage Merlin bombers was a drop tank beneath each mainplane featured here by LR500 in May 1943. After ten months service with 109 Squadron the aircraft served with 105 Squadron from March 1944 to the end of hostilities* (de Havilland).

Above right *DZ540 was converted into the prototype PR Mk XVI, powered by Merlin 72/73 engines. It is portrayed in Dark Green and Dark Earth, with yellow under surfaces and P marking which is partly outlined black. The serials and spinners were also black. It was recorded as depicted, with cockpit canopy bulges and fixed radio mast, at RAE Farnborough on September 30 1944. DZ540 first flew in the summer of 1943 and went to A&AEE late August for performance, handling and pressure cabin tests. Performance testing showed it to have a service ceiling of 36,000 ft, top speed in Full Supercharger gear of 401 mph TAS at 25,000 ft and a cruising speed of 366 mph TAS at 30,600 ft. It was returned to Hatfield for overhaul in July 1944 then was passed to RAE Farnborough. It was struck off charge on July 28 1945.*

Right *NS997/G was an FB Mk VI of 169 Squadron. Many 100 Group Mosquitoes featured black under surfaces, yet not all as evidenced by VI:C recorded on March 11 1945 after its AI Mk V radar had been removed. Its finish is Dark Green and Medium Sea Grey with red codes and black serials. Although it joined A Flight 169 Squadron on March 28 1944, it was June before the squadron operated Mk IVs and from Great Massingham. On July 23 1944 NS997/G shot down a Bf 110 during bomber support operations against Kiel. From September intruders and Day Rangers were flown. When Mk XIXs re-equipped the squadron in February 1945 NS997/G reached Cambridge for overhaul passing into storage at 273 MU in October 1945. It escaped destruction and, via 37 MU Burtonwood and 38 MU Llandow, was flown to the Yugoslav Air Force in April 1952.*

respects one might compare these forays with those of the night nuisance Mosquitoes. But the Fw 190 was ill-equipped for such use and navigation was a major problem for the German pilots whose single bomb could not compare with the loads which the faster, higher-flying Mosquitoes would soon be delivering to Germany — and in quantity. The Mosquito XIIs of 85 Squadron in particular took on the 190s, after the Typhoons had proved too slow and too ill-equipped to be of much use. On May 16/17 85 Squadron shot down four FW 190s and were proving to be the masters, and at a time when one of the most spectacular bombing campaigns of the war was coming to a close.

The start of 1943 had seen the Mosquito day bomber really in its stride although winter weather curtailed operations. Then came the excitement of January 30 when both Goebbels and Goering addressed their countrymen. At a rally in Berlin, Goering the German Air Force leader, whose boast about no enemy aeroplanes invading the Reich was already shattered, would be totally humiliated by the aeroplane of good chance. At breakfast time in England four Mosquitoes of 105 Squadron, led by the famed Squadron Leader R. W.

Reynolds, set off to punish the German boaster. As intended their arrival over Berlin coincided with Goering's proposed activity. Amid muffles the German radio announced a temporary hitch in the broadcast which was put off for an hour . . . to the utter delight of informed British listeners. It goes without saying that the four Mosquitoes bombed Berlin — in daylight — and came home safely.

Then it was the turn of 139 Squadron whose target was the muttering of Herr Goebbels. One can imagine the fury of the German leadership, whose angry response doubtless cost 139 Squadron its last man 'in', Squadron Leader D.F.W. Darling.

There was more to the raid than mere propaganda value for, yet again, it bequeathed to the British very useful flight profile information for Berlin raids, and the possible loads the aircraft could carry.

February and March 1943 were months during which many Mosquito day raids were mounted, often to targets quite deep in enemy territory. On March 3 it was the molybdenum mine at Knaben, Norway, that met the fury of nine Mosquitoes of 139 Squadron led by Wing Commander Peter Shand, after a sea crossing demand-

ing great flying skill and very accurate navigation. To ensure that the correct crossing points on the Norwegian coast could be found Coastal Command, in May 1943, formed a special flight in 333(Norwegian) Squadron whose crews could act as navigation leaders on strike missions and fly reconnaissances along the coast.

To penetrate Germany in daylight, as the Americans were daily finding, was costly and horrific. On March 16 105 and 139 Squadrons showed that it was well within their capability when they raided the railway installations at Paderborn, their deepest low-level penetration yet. Rail targets commonly figured in the operations orders of the two squadrons at this time, and on March 23 it was the railway workshops at Nantes which were singled out for attack. Every effort was made to ensure that attacks against targets in occupied territory would bring the smallest number of civilian casualties, and in this respect the Nantes raid was typical.

Again led by Peter Shand, with Flight Lieutenant W. C. S. Blessing — so long a Mosquito personality — the attack was timed to take place precisely as one shift of workers left the factory and others were about to clock on, the works being briefly empty of French personnel. Such precision attacks demanded infinite skill in routing, timing and sheer brilliant flying, for Nantes is some way from Marham. In a manner quite unequalled in any but Mosquito operations the crews swept into the attack exactly as planned. Such precision was nothing new, for when Eindhoven was bombed in December 1942 the raid was timed for 12.30 hrs GMT. As the Mosquito force went in a photographer took a shot of a clock tower in Eindhoven, to prove that the Mosquitoes, and indeed 2 Group, were right on time.

As May 1943 drew to a close Marham's residents were driven into a state of shock. Certainly the day raids had not been without loss. Considering the venturesome nature of many of them, and the constant dangers of low flying, it was surprising that the loss rate of around 7 per cent was not higher. But it was not losses that brought about an end to the pernicious, stinging

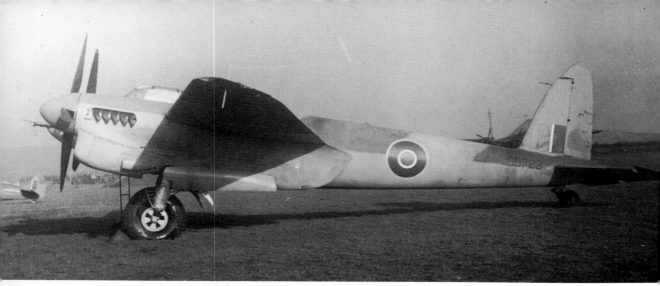

Mosquito NF II DD723 was fitted with Lancaster power units experimentally at Rolls-Royce in the latter half of 1943. Previously it had served with 85 Squadron and ended its life at Cambridge early in 1945 (Rolls-Royce).

Mosquito raids. It was a very different policy decision by the Staff at Bomber Command.

That decision had already been taken when the last Mosquito day bomber raid was mounted, one which proved to be the deepest daylight low-level penetration during this phase of the Mosquito's career. 139 Squadron's six crews attacked the Schott glass works at Jena whilst eight crews of 105 Squadron had as their target the famous Zeiss optics factory, also at Jena. It was a splendid operation with which to round off one of the most glorious phases in RAF history, one of the most spectacular and indelible.

The day of the Mosquito bomber was all but ended for Bomber Command had decided that the aircraft could more usefully be employed in a night nuisance bombing campaign, as a night marker force and that Mosquitoes in 192 Squadron based at Feltwell would undertake radio warfare. They would snoop upon radio and radar transmissions in a very secret war and use Mosquitoes to the close of hostilities, being the last squadron to take the Mk IV into action.

A particular niche which the Mosquitoes would also fill to the end of the war was that of long-range meteorological reconnaissance through enemy air space. The first Mk IV for the task was delivered to 1401 Flight of Coastal Command in April 1942. Weather reconnaissance flights began from Bircham Newton in July, the task being to gather details of weather conditions ahead of Bomber Command operations. In August 1942 the flight became 521 Squadron with an increased establishment for Mosquitoes which, by the autumn, were flying very deep sorties into Europe. This phase of operations ended on March 31 1943 when the Mosquitoes were all passed to Bomber Command's 1409 Flight at Oakington where its first Mk IXs arrived in May.

Mid-summer was an increasingly taxing time for Mosquito fighter crews. Additional Instep sorties were flown as enemy interference with Coastal Command aircraft over Biscay was greater. In the Middle East 23 Squadron, now using FB VIs, some of the first in service, was carrying out a highly active and fruitful intruding campaign, particularly over southern Italy, as the Services prepared for the Sicilian adventure. At home the fighters faced a new, faster quarry in the Messerschmitt Me 410 which first appeared over Britain in June 1943. It had a top speed of 388 mph at 21,980 ft and so was marginally faster than the early Mosquito fighter. It was well armed too, with two forward-firing 20 mm cannon and two 7.9 mm machine-guns. It had two barbettes on the rear fuselage each mounting two 13 mm MG 131s. The ammunition runs were an unfortunate design feature, for many Me 410s disintegrated when the ammunition runs were ignited. The Me 410 could also carry about a 500 kg bomb load, and thus was very useful as a fast intruder. The first Me 410 shot down by a Mosquito fell into the sea off Felixstowe on July 13/14 1943. During the month following Me 410s of KG 2 became quite active at night, filtering into returning bomber streams and attempting high-level bombing raids on airfields. Fortunately for Bomber Command the Luftwaffe was unable to sustain such activities, and Mosquitoes shot down quite a high proportion of the relatively few Me 410s in service.

The PR Mk IX was now in service, 540 Squadron having taken delivery of the first examples in May 1943. Such was its supremacy that not one was lost in action until October 1943. The value of the PR IX became very apparent when, during the late spring and into summer, an intensified watch was mounted upon the V-weapons establishment at Peenemünde. After the famous August raid on the research station it was PR IX LR413 which brought home photographic evidence of the effectiveness of the attack.

If the Mosquito was to live up to the maker's claims

and fit the official requirements it had to be able to operate overseas where heat and high humidity might play havoc with a wooden structure, not to mention the glue involved. Late in 1942 two Mk IIs were sent to the Middle East to find whether they could stand up to the conditions. They were held by 60 Squadron, South African Air Force to be picketted out. But the temptation to fly them was too great to overcome. The squadron installed cameras and managed to get the Mosquitoes operating by February 1943, the same month as 683 (PR) Squadron formed at Luqa, Malta, using Mosquitoes, initially some IIs and later IVs and IXs.

Two Mosquito IIs were also sent to the Far East for acclimatisation trials, in an area in which, although the Mosquito was to give good and lengthy service, it was never at its very best because of weather conditions and insect attacks on both the resin and the wooden structure.

In the Middle East there was need for every available aircraft to assist with the invasion of Sicily, the stepping stone for Italy. To assist and much increase the viability of the night fighter force in the Mediterranean area part of 256 Squadron was detached to join 108 Squadron. This addition of AI VIII equipped aircraft brought rapid dividends, and the remainder of the squadron was released from Fighter Command to join the detachment in October 1943.

The possibility of extending the use of Mosquitoes overseas was further advanced when the first Australian-built example, A52-1, first flew on July 23 1943. This was indeed a milestone. To achieve it Merlin engines had to be taken to Australia, likewise many components. It was decided that production should, for a start anyway, be devoted to the fighter-bomber Mosquito and that American-built Packard Merlins should be fitted to these aircraft. The first example flew merely a year after the initial sets of drawings reached Sydney, flown via the Atlantic Ferry Service in a Liberator. In December 1952 the Mk II DD664 began flying again after being sent to Australia by sea. It was two Merlin 31s from this machine that powered A52-1 on its maiden flight.

July 1943 also saw the arrival of Mk VIs on 605 Squadron at Castle Camps. This squadron, together with 418, was to be busily engaged on very deep Ranger and intruder missions over Europe during the next six months. It was not only these exciting and rewarding operations that would make the County of Warwick's contribution to the Mosquito story memorable. Using Mosquitoes at night 605 Squadron's crews were particularly shocked at the large number of RAF bombers they saw fall prey during night raids. The commanding officer of 605 Squadron at one time suggested that bombers tow bombs to keep enemy fighters well away, but the best answer lay within his hands — the Mosquito.

Employing Mosquitoes in any form of night escort role was impossible, but by slowly developing suitable tactics, which 605 Squadron was exploring by August 1943, the Mosquitoes could be skilfully deployed during night operations to engage night fighters although this stage in the Mosquito story belongs more to 1944 than 1943. The Fighter Interception Unit at Ford fitted rearward-looking radar which would enable a Mosquito

The application of two-stage Merlin engines greatly enhanced the capability of reconnaissance Mosquitoes like the PR IX LR409 depicted at Hatfield in June 1943 prior to overseas service.

to pick out a tailing fighter and quickly turn to take up position behind the enemy.

Summer months saw the gradual extension of the Mosquito into the Far East war. Two Mosquitoes joined 681 Squadron at Dum Dum, photo-reconnaissance operations were commenced and the first Mk VIs arrived in India. The plan was for seven squadrons of Mosquitoes to operate in the Far East. In September the first two PR IXs reached India where 684 Squadron already held a few Mk IIIs and VIs for reconnaissance purposes before equipping with IXs at a later date.

Each month some new aspect to the Mosquito's career emerged, and none more so than in October 1943. 544 Squadron had just commenced active service and was already flying very deep penetration missions — to Rechlin, the German aircraft test centre, and to Berlin for photographs upon which the massive Battle of Berlin would be based.

It was in October that the fighter-bomber Mk XVIII powered by Merlin 25s to afford a good low-level performance and able to fire 25 six-pounder shells in 20 seconds and carry, as an alternative, wing bombs or eight 60 lb rockets, came into service. Soon 248 Squadron would be using them for ocean patrol and attack duties, although U-boats were destined not to be the main targets after all. It was at this period that Mk XVIs started to leave the production lines, their pressure cabins fitting them well for photo-reconnaissance now made all the more dangerous because the German jet fighters were not all that far from active service. Mosquitoes of 140 Squadron began their tactical reconnaissance task in which they would take millions of photographs of northern France in preparation for the invasion. They also came across the first flying-bomb sites being prepared in France.

The necessity of ever maintaining a fast and technically advanced night fighter force was demonstrated when, in October, the new Ju 188s of KG 6 engaged in attempts to bomb London. This fast version of the ubiquitous Ju 88, the nearest German equivalent to the Mosquito, relied upon *Düppel* for cover. This was the German version of Window and was intended to jam British ground and airborne radars. The small number of German bombers operated, however, meant that the metal strips afforded little protection. There was, nevertheless, much concern about the ease with which the Mosquitoes' radar could be confused. These raiders came in high, dived fast and flew home quite low, their time over Britain being brief, especially so when compared with the lengthy sorties over Germany now being flown at night by Mosquito bombers of 105 and 139 Squadrons. Whereas the Luftwaffe bombers were bombing wide, the Mosquitoes were attacking precision targets with some success at night.

With the introduction of the Me 410, Ju 188 and refined versions of the Do 217 the German bomber force slightly increased its activity. Against this the Mosquito night force comprised the Mk II with AI V, Mk XII equivalent to the Mk II but with AI VIII and the Mk XVII with American radar. Coming along was the Mk XIX with American radar and Merlin 25s to boost low level performance. The Mk XIII with improved radar and the wing built initially for the Mk VI fighter-bomber which also permitted it to carry wing drop tanks, was also in service. The first success with the Mk XIII came to 488 Squadron in November 1943.

It was now very clear that future fighter development would need to boost the Mosquito's climb ability and increase its speed at around 20,000 ft and above; heights at which enemy bombers were now operating. This meant the installation of the more powerful two-stage Merlin engines. For the present some improvement in performance was being attained by paying a lot of attention to detail, such as the sealing of oil leaks, making sure cowling panels fitted well, and so on.

October 1943 has also come to be remembered for one particular operation, a landmark in the Mosquito's career for it was made by squadrons of 2 Group — now part of the Tactical Air Force. That assortment of courageous men whose numbers were savagely reduced in 1940 and 1941, and by whom the Mosquito bomber had been pioneered, would once more take their favourite mount into action. They would do so just as the widespread ascendancy of the Mosquito over all other bomber types was clear for all to witness.

The day chosen by 2 Group to re-enter the Mosquito stakes was October 3 1943, and Mk VI fighter-bombers of 456 and 487 Squadrons did so in style so typical of this Group. This is hardly surprising for aboard one of the Mosquitoes was a certain Wing Commander Smith who was flying despite all orders prohibiting a senior officer from taking part in operations. Beneath the disguise was none other than Air Vice-Marshal Basil Embry, surely one of the greatest RAF characters of all time and one of the boldest. He was not alone for with him was David Atcherley, one of the Atcherley twins whose humerous contributions to air force life can surely never be forgotten. Only an Atcherley could have slipped into line a few moments ahead of Field Marshal Montgomery to take the cheers of the inhabitants of Brussels upon its liberation.

On the occasion of the October raid David Atcherley was flying strictly unofficially, for he had a broken arm. An arm in a sling, and a few nasty official orders, these were not the stuff to ground 2 Group's most popular and colourful characters. But behind this lay immense courage and brilliant leadership qualities. In the Mosquito, Basil Embry and 'Batchy' had found their ideal aeroplane, and with it they intended to win the war. What a splendid and unique combination!

The first Mosquito fighter-bomber Wing was based at Sculthorpe in Norfolk, so that operations over France needed to take place from an advanced base. This situation had come about because Bomber Command took back from 2 Group some of its bases in the summer of 1943, and the tactical formations had to be placed where airfields were available on a temporary basis. Thus it was that the Mosquitoes of 464 and 487 Squadrons flew to Exeter early on October 3, to be suitably placed for the foray.

Around midday they set off on the first of thousands of sorties using the Mk VI which would be as effective as they would often be spectacular. Their targets, which they attacked from low levels, were power stations deep in France, and they employed tactics akin to those used previously by 2 Group. It was soon apparent that, as ever, to be effective such attacks needed to be thoroughly well thought-out. By the end of 1943 Lo-Hi-Lo profile operations were being mounted — and in haste — for the V1 sites in France had to be wiped out if a pernicious new offensive was to be stopped. To be nearer the scene of operations and to permit many more sorties to be flown, the fighter-bomber Wing moved to Hunsdon, near Bishop's Stortford.

The tempo of Mosquito employment was expanding fast. In November 1943 627 Squadron formed, equipped with some spare Mk IVs. Its role was as a bomber squadron whose targets would be lit by flares from 139 Squadron which was switched to an almost exclusively marking role. Between them these two squadrons formed the nucleus of a special light night bomber striking force which in 1943 remained in its infancy.

Equally important, the closing weeks of 1943 saw the establishment of 100 Group and its commencement of operations. This was the formation which would try to intercept, or at least discourage, enemy night fighters attacking RAF bombers. This task needed considerable skill and elaborate planning to achieve worthwhile results. Initially 100 Group squadrons relied upon aged Mosquito IIs with out-dated radar, used for fear the aircraft might come down in enemy territory where the capture of AI Mk VIII or SCR720 might give too much away. The first bomber support sorties were flown by Mosquitoes of 141 Squadron which had already pioneered such sorties with their Serrate-equipped Beaufighters.

As if these major trends were insufficient, 248 Squadron in Coastal Command commenced to equip with Mosquito VIs in December, and would use these in strike duties against shipping.

Thus, 1943 had been a year of expanding Mosquito operations, careful development and production of important new variants. Mosquitoes were in use in almost every conceivable operational manner. Mosquito airliners were on the Swedish route, Mosquitoes were watching over almost the whole of Europe despite the very long distances involved, and were making long, deep penetrations in daylight. By day too they were intruding upon even central European airfields. No mean achievement for the unwanted miracle.

Chapter Five

The final fling

The fighter-bomber campaign swung into rapid ferocity, with 2 Group's Mk VIs sweeping low across the flying-bomb sites and later using specialised shallow dive tactics to become the most effective unit in destroying this potent danger. Meanwhile the Mosquito night bomber offensive was also gathering momentum.

By pure chance October 3 1943, which saw those fighter-bombers roar into action, was also the date when the leading Mosquito night bomber squadron, 139, took Mk IXs into action for the first time during a Hanover raid. Such operations had hitherto been merely nuisance attacks. Now that Bomber Command was very strong, and the enemy fighter force equally strengthened, new uses were being sought for the Command's Mosquitoes. They would now fly diversion or 'spoof' raids to mislead the enemy as to the night's main targets, and drop large quantities of Window ahead of operations.

It was not long before the Mosquito force expanded in two ways. Firstly, the number of squadrons increased and, in February 1944, 692 Squadron commenced operations. Secondly, the arrival of the first Mk XXs — similar to the Mk IV but built in Canada and usually equipped for service at 13 Maintenance Unit, Henlow, provided a useful second supply source. The newcomer was first taken into action on December 2 1943 by 139 Squadron. Whereas previously this squadron had been led into action by Oboe squadrons, 139 now began marking for the new Light Night Striking Force (LNSF) of 8 Group and, at the turn of the year, was testing Gee-H.

Early weeks of 1944 were a turning point in the Mosquito story for another reason. It will be recalled that since 1943 attempts had been made to enable the Mosquito to deliver a 4,000 lb 'cookie'. Installation of the weapon posed few problems but, in flight, both Mosquito IVs and IXs thus armed became inherently unstable. There was little that could be done to cure the problem. Provided that crews exercised caution, operations were quite safe and so, on February 23 1944, it fell to three crews of 692 Squadron to take the Mosquito IV with the 'big bomb' into action, the target being Düsseldorf. It was a tremendous achievement for a light bomber to be able to deliver such a weapon. Coupled with the available speed it would be possible, in theory, for each Mosquito to deliver at least two such weapons during two sorties within one night.

With expansion of the LNSF underway, 627 Squadron departed to join 5 Group as a special marker squadron whose activities became closely linked with 617 Squadron, the Dam Busters. The LNSF's effective strength had increased because of the arrival of the B Mk XVI which had been planned from the start to carry a 'cookie' and not suffer from stability problems. Mark XVIs entered service as the Germans were deploying specially devised 'anti-Mosquito' flak, effective to 40,000 ft. Mosquitoes of LNSF were damaged more by predicted flak than fighter interception. Sometimes the night bombers flew through intensive barrages.

In April 1944 571 Squadron began operating with B XVIs and 139 Squadron had some of its Mk XXs fitted with H_2S in their noses. The ever-ubiquitous nature of the Mosquito was revealed anew in May 1944 when, flying low, aircraft of 692 Squadron mined the Kiel Canal.

Bomber Command's 100 Group formed on November 8 1943 gathering under its jurisdiction various bomber support and electronic warfare units which were gradually forming into an extensive force. Fighter Command squadrons from time to time participated in night bomber support roles whilst remaining in their parent Command. 25 Squadron, for instance, had begun simple bomber support operations with its Mosquitoes as early as May 1943 and from August used Mk VIs. Later that year 456 Squadron began taking part in Mahmoud sorties during which the Mosquito would be flown to one of a number of specially chosen points

A Mosquito FB Mk VI of 418 (RCAF) Squadron undergoing overhaul and re-arming.

Mosquito B XXV KB490 replaced DZ650 as AZ:Q in 627 Squadron on January 20 1945, after arriving at 13 MU Henlow from Canada on December 30 1944. It was one of a handful of Mk XXVs with swollen bomb-bays to accommodate the 4,000 lb bomb. The Dull Red codes outlined in yellow on the Ocean Grey—Dark Green—Medium Sea Grey finish were typical of 5 Group late in the war. So were identical letters applied on the top of the tailplane. It was recorded at Cambridge on June 17 1945 when fitted with paddle-bladed propellers and having the outline in black of a nude on the nose flanked by 50 operation symbols in yellow including one to depict mining and one the dropping of a 'cookie'. KB490 passed to 109 Squadron in October 1945 then went into storage at Little Snoring in April 1946. It was struck off charge at 51 MU on November 7 1947.

over enemy territory known to be assembly points for German night fighters. On November 3 1943, 141 Squadron became operational, the first Mosquito fighter squadron in Bomber Command, and equipped with Serrate fitted into Mosquito IIs which were readily identifiable as serving in 100 Group by their black under surfaces. Next came 239 and 169 Squadrons which began operations in January 1944. Initially these night fighters were employed in three phase operations, i) in the target area during or after main force attack, ii) to engage night fighters at their assembly points, or iii) by flying some eight minutes away from the bomber stream there to pick off night interceptors. The Mosquito IIs were aged now, like their radar, and in an attempt to improve performance many were fitted with Merlin XXII engines. Some Mk VIs became available in the spring.

By May 1944 there were 100 Mosquitoes in 100 Group, mostly Mk IIs. Therefore 85 and 157 Squadrons were drafted into Bomber Command then equipped with NF Mk XIXs fitted with AI Mk X centimetric radar, which had been released for use over enemy territory on April 21 1944. The value of the Mosquitoes in 100 Group was probably less at this time than might have been the case, for much of Bomber Command's activity was then over occupied territories close at hand and not within night fighter defended areas in Germany.

Mosquito Mk XX KB162 named 'New Glasgow' was the first Canadian Mosquito to cross the Atlantic for the RAF, and arrived in Britain in August 1943. It served with 139 Squadron as XD:J from December 1943 until it crashed at Warboys on October 14 1944 as a result of engine failure on take-off (de Havilland).

The Mosquitoes therefore tended to conduct their operations more along the lines of modified intruder activity.

Home-based night fighter squadrons became slightly busier late in 1943, then, on January 21/22 1944, there was a sudden upsurge of enemy activity. As a reply to the RAF's mighty raids on Berlin a motley collection of the Luftwaffe's modern bombers opened a mini-Blitz on London and a few other British cities. Despite a display of techniques far superior to any previously employed, in the Luftwaffe's two-wave raid only one fifth of the bombers despatched reached the capital. Nine enemy aircraft were shot down and, to a Mosquito of 151 Squadron, fell the prize of the night — the first He 177 four-engined bomber to fall in Britain.

In February eight night raids were directed against London, the most successful coming on February 18.

Düppel gave some protection to the raiders, but searchlights helped to neutralise the effect of the metal foil strips and Mosquitoes shot down a number of enemy aircraft. During March 1944 the London raids faded out as the enemy turned to Hull, Norwich and Bristol, all defended by a collection of Mosquito NF XIIs, XIIIs and XVIIs. Although quite protracted, the German campaign scale declined fast. The enemy was in no state to maintain his effort, and the mini-Blitz ended on May 29 1944. Luckily, too, for the Allies needed maximum night fighter cover for their invasion.

Fighter Command divided at the end of 1943 so that 10½ squadrons joined ADGB leaving the other night fighter squadrons to join 85 Group. By D-Day six Mosquito squadrons of 85 Group were on hand to protect invasion forces from night marauders leaving another seven squadrons and the Fighter Interception Unit to provide home defence.

Things were slowly changing in Coastal Command too. At the start of 1944 they had 248 Squadron training to use Mosquito VIs for fighter-reconnaissance and strike support. Operations commenced on February 20 1944 and they included ocean patrols off South-West England, Ju 88 interceptions over Biscay and strike support for the Mosquito XVIIIs. These roles 248 Squadron maintained until after the Normandy landings, for Coastal Command was still relying on Beaufighters for strike duties because Mosquito VIs were earmarked for more pressing situations.

During the five months prior to the invasion thousands of Mosquito sorties were flown, by day and night, over France to gather photographs vital to the forthcoming invasion campaign. 140 and 544 Squadrons watched the building of the V-weapons sites, returning with photographs for TAF briefings. Many operations were at low level or employed shallow dive which meant flying towards very heavy defences with no means of silencing them. Three Mosquito PR squadrons, 4, 140 and 400 in 2 TAF, concentrated upon gathering further photographs for invasion planning.

In February 1944 PR XVIs commenced operating, and the first clear photographs of Berlin — now being savaged by the heavy bombers — were obtained.

Small in strength, mighty in import, was the specialised 1409 Flight whose Wyton-based Mosquito IXs and XVIs gathered information daily on the weather over the whole of Europe ahead of Allied air operations. These were risky, lengthy ventures into very hostile areas. When the invasion of France was set 1409 Meteorological Flight was active assessing the weather situation in preparation for the order for the invasion to commence. The Flight's Mosquitoes also had another specialised role, that of flying ahead of VIPs to ensure that weather conditions would afford them safe and comfortable passage. Such work continued until well after the war.

If one Mark of Mosquito is looked upon as contributing most to that aircraft's popular image it must be the Mk VI. At the start of 1944 fighter-bomber VIs of 2 Group were attacking the V-weapons sites, indulging in some night bomber support and interdictor work which afforded training for the highly intensive intruder campaign to follow the D-Day landings and, for everyone's encouragement, a few highly spectacular daylight missions against pin-point targets.

Barely had the first fight-bomber Wing formed when the second, led by 613 Squadron, came into being at Lasham. Air Marshal Sir Basil Embry's desire to see 2 Group in constant battle took 21 Squadron on to Day Ranger flights in November 1943 and 464 Squadron practising night attacks on airfields in December 1943. During January 1944 four squadrons, 21, 464, 487 and 613, were engaged upon attacking V1 sites, for which purpose 107 and 305 Squadrons equipped with Mosquitoes and joined the Lasham Wing in February 1944. These Mosquitoes operated in packs of four, six or eight and flew fast and low in one-pass raids on the flying-bomb sites. It was dangerous, for there could often be crowding during the fast run in and, for safety's sake and accuracy, the Mosquitoes were soon attacking in pairs or fours.

The first of the second round of Mosquito 'spectaculars' took place on February 18 1944 when a precision attack was needed in order to blast a hole in the wall of the prison at Amiens. This task was allotted to the Hunsdon Wing and, to boost morale after an accident, 487 Squadron was chosen to lead with the famed Group Captain P.C. Pickard flying HX922:EG-F. With crews

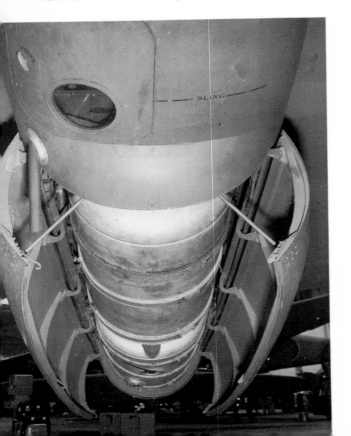

SLING

from 21 and 464 Squadrons to the rear, each allotted a specific role, the Mosquitoes flew in low over snow surfaced France to deliver one of the most famous raids of the war. It also involved probably the most successful Mosquito of all, the famed 'O Orange'—DZ414. This was the aircraft which repeatedly snooped upon the enemy from Norway to North Africa and often deep into eastern Europe, which took a vast number of photographs before and after many special operations.

Hunsdon Wing went into action again, on March 18 1944, the target being the Hazemeyer electrics factory at Hengelo. The nature of the target brought less recognition of the attack than that on Amiens prison. The third 'spectacular' came on April 11 1944, when six crews of 613 Squadron made an attack on the Dutch Central Population Registry in the Hague using a mixture of HE 500 lb and incendiary bombs. The nearby Peace Palace was to be undamaged at all costs, and this demanded an attack of extreme accuracy such as the Mosquito squadrons had become well known for. In the event the precise building was felled with little damage to the area around. Within this period of the war there were other specialised low-level raids on communications targets such as the rail centres at Hirson, Haine St Pierre and Ghislain.

The possibility of using Mosquitoes as pattern bombers after the style of the USAAF's Marauders was attempted with Mk VIs whose crews bombed upon markers placed by Oboe-guided Mosquitoes. The air-craft were unsuitable for such tactics, the Mk VIs being better employed in low-level attacks on coastal radar sites, coastal guns and radio stations, all of which needed to be neutralised before the invasion fleet headed for Normandy.

By June 1944 the basic Mosquito development programme was complete, for the two-stage Merlin bomber and PR aircraft were in service. Future development would be along the lines of increased range and modified power plants. A two-stage engined fighter had still to enter service, and this had emerged as the Mk XXX based upon the Mk XIX's airframes. Prior to the spring of 1944 there was still little need for such an aircraft, and it was therefore not introduced on production lines for fear of causing too much of an interruption to Mk VI and night fighter production.

Barely had the new version begun to leave the factory when the old familiar exhaust shroud burning problems arose, just as the invasion was about to take place. There was delay before the Mk XXX became generally available and it was many months before it was a going concern.

The Normandy invasion brought a rapid upsurge in Mosquito night fighter activity, but it was the fighter-bomber VIs which became busiest of all. The 2 TAF squadrons were in action along such lines from the moment the invasion was launched. Sometimes guided by flares dropped by Mitchells, the Mosquito fighter-

Left *In its swollen bomb-bay the Mosquito carried a 4,000 lb bomb. Its reconnaissance equivalent carried tankage sufficient even for nine-hour sorties.* (de Havilland).

Right *Mosquito NF XXX MM695/G, an early production example, operated with 219 Squadron between July 1944 and March 1945 when it became ZQ:Z at CFE Tangmere.*

Below *HK415 KP:R stands by a block of farm buildings — which, upon close scrutiny, turn out to be a disguised hangar* (R.H. Finlayson).

bombers' crews kept an eye upon every movement around the battlefields of Normandy from dusk to dawn virtually preventing the Germans from moving troops at night. Gradually, the area under their surveillance widened as, each night, Mosquitoes were given rectangular areas within which to patrol. When finally the Germans were dislodged from Normandy the Mk VI squadrons pestered their withdrawal — particularly as they headed for the Seine crossing points. Vast amounts of ammunition were expended during ground attacks, and on virtually anything that moved on any night in the prescribed areas.

When the situation demanded it, specialised low-level attacks continued to be delivered, as on June 10 when petrol tankers were gathered at Chatellerault, and on the barracks at Poitiers, also on a school building housing Germans at Egeltons and the SS headquarters at Vincey.

Moderate-scale night attacks were made by the Luftwaffe on Allied forces in the lodgement area during June 1944 and this brought action for the Mosquito squadrons of 85 Group. Then came the appearance in British skies of V-1 flying-bombs in mid-June 1944. Perhaps unexpectedly it was a Mosquito VI of 605 Squadron which at night on June 15 1944 scored the first Mosquito success against a V-1. As soon as the salvo firing of V-1s came underway 96, 219, 409 and 418 Squadrons were put on to anti-diver night patrols. Flying-bombs flew as fast as Mosquitoes in level flight, so that catching them usually meant a dive attack. Successfully intercepting them was far from easy for their small cross-section was not easy to follow on AI

radar carried by the Mosquito XIIIs. Therefore 85 and 157 Squadrons' Mk XIXs were recalled from Bomber Command to enter the anti-V-1 campaign. By mid-July 1944 there were nine Mosquito fighter squadrons operating against the V-1s. The success rate was quite high, but interception of the flying-bombs was difficult on cloudy nights. During August 1944 418 Squadron achieved a success rate of about one flying-bomb per day. The top-scoring pilot was Squadron Leader Russ Bannock, credited with 18½ V-1s. A total of 471 V-1s were claimed by the seven full-time anti-'diver' squadrons, and 152 by the part-timers.

A new side to the V-1 campaign appeared with the first launch of a flying-bomb from a Heinkel He 111 of KG 3 from over the North Sea on July 8 1944. Nearly all such launches would be by night, and from aircraft flying very low and releasing their weapons about 50 miles off shore. The launch Heinkels were obvious targets, but catching them proved difficult because, by flying very low, they had a tactical advantage little lessened by the use of standing patrols and primitive 'look down' radar. This situation persisted right to the end of their campaign late in the war.

By a month after D-Day night fighters of 85 Group had claimed 100 enemy aircraft, and within days a second squadron had received Mk XXXs. 219 Squadron had received XXXs first, beginning on June 13 1944, and were already encountering exhaust problems although this did not prevent 406 Squadron, the second to use them, from operating Mk XXXs in July.

There was another problem too with the Mk XXX for

Below left Very clearly evident here — the thimble nose radome on HK425, which carries a polecat emblem on the nose. Photograph taken at Twente (R.H. Finlayson).

Below right Late in the war some Mosquitoes of 100 Group were fitted with ASH radar originally to be carried in a container on a wing bomb rack. PZ4593 P:Q seen at Little Snoring in 1945 has ASH in a small nose radome (M. G. Williams).

Below far right The ability of the Mosquito to absorb tremendous punishment and survive is well shown here, HK425 KP:D of 409 (RCAF) Squadron having had much of the port tailplane shot away, as well as a flap, during December 1944 (R.H. Finlayson).

NF Mk XXX MT487 ZK:L wore the usual grey-green night fighter camouflage. Delivered to 218 MU on September 28 1944, it reached 25 Squadron at Castle Camps on October 6 1944 as the squadron re-equipped with Mk XXXs. These aircraft were from December 1944 used for intruder patrols. Bomber support operations began on February 1 1945 and MT487 took part in 25 Squadron's final wartime operation, a night ranger to German airfields, on April 25 1945. It left 25 Squadron in February 1946 for Marshall's of Cambridge where it was scrapped soon after.

its exhausts glowed very brightly and this was a grave disadvantage for any night flier. By the close of 1944 seven squadrons had Mk XXXs, whose main use came during bomber support operations in which 11 and 12 Groups operated along the lines of 100 Group's squadrons.

Mosquitoes of 100 Bomber Support Group were fast increasing their kill rates. 85 and 157 Squadrons had begun a phase in 100 Group's war in June 1944 by flying low-level patrols over enemy airfields, operations backed by Mk VIs carrying bombs and designed to prohibit German night fighters from taking off. The second phase involved picking off the first enemy fighters to get airborne. The third phase would be a

patrol in areas of likely German night fighter activity about 30 minutes after the bombers had cleared the region.

23 Squadron returned from the Mediterranean Theatre in July 1944 with an illustrious intruder record, re-equipped with Mk VIs and joined 100 Group. The following month 141 Squadron at last changed its Mk IIs for VIs and during 1944 the Mk II was finally phased out of 100 Group's squadrons. This came at a time of much advance in radio warfare and constant changes in radio and radar equipment.

An interesting feature of the bomber-support Mosquitoes of 23, 141 and 515 Squadrons was the fitting in the nose tip of Mk X ASH radar placed in a small

cylindrical dome on the Mosquito VIs. This meant that the Mk VI fighter-bomber could now take its place as a night fighter. By the end of 1944 Mosquitoes of 100 Group were mounting spoof raids on German cities and Mosquito XXXs were in service in the Group's squadrons. The combination of 100 Group and the LNSF meant that it was possible some nights to have the whole of Germany under air raid alert — and sometimes this was brought about by a handful of Mosquitoes tracking widely over Germany and causing utter confusion. No armed heavies could possibly have achieved that — and with impunity. Before the war ended 100 Group switched to a fire-raising offensive against the remaining German airfields by dropping incendiaries and napalm on to the last Luftwaffe outposts.

Almost to the end of hostilities in Europe reconnaissance Mosquitoes photographed the shrinking Nazi domain. On July 9 1944 one of these aircraft made the longest duration flight, of 7 hours 45 minutes, by a Mosquito in the European conflict during a flight to the Narvik area. This was at a time when the USAAF was using Mosquitoes for weather scouting, for night reconnaissance sorties or as navigation leaders. The

Mosquitoes were of the 25th Bomb Group based at Watton. Others used by the Americans were in the 492nd Bomb Group which flew operations to aid the Resistance forces in Europe.

It was a foregone conclusion that, sooner or later, PR Mosquitoes would come face to face with German jet fighters. That misfortune fell to a crew of 544 Squadron on July 25 1944 when an Me 262 was encountered. For all its speed the German jet was outmanoeuvred by the Mosquito, which would prove time and again to be the case in such situations. Manoeuvreability more than pure speed brought safety to Mosquitoes faced with Me 163s and 262s.

Some element of safety for PR crews came about when the very high flier, the PR Mk 32 with increased wing span, entered service. A trials aircraft for the new configuration, MM328, was tested early in 1944. Five production PR 32s followed, being built in August 1944. These could reach heights of up to 42,000 ft because of a reduction in all-up weight by the removal of some equipment, and it added 30 mph to their operational speed. The first operation using a PR 32 took place on December 5 1944, the new version coming into service as the Me 163 and 262 were being more frequently encountered. All was not well with the PR 32 for some time, for there was canopy icing and also cockpit heating problems.

At the other extreme were a handful of specially modified low-flying PR Mosquitoes, some of which had nose-mounted F24 cameras, or an F24 fitted in the front of each wing drop tank. This made these aircraft ideal for photography whilst diving at a target. A handful of Mk VIs were modified in like manner. With engines better rated for low flying, and retention of armament, such aircraft were even more effective than the PR IXs.

Photographic reconnaissance was a role featured by Mosquitoes in the Mediterranean area to the close of the war, and many such sorties were flown by crews of 60 Squadron, South African Air Force. They achieved some very deep penetration flights, to Poland to keep a watch on V2 activities, over southern Europe, the Balkans and Austria. By the latter part of 1944 P-51 Mustangs afforded support to the hitherto lone fliers, for jet activity was interfering with the PR IXs and XVIs which were being used in a similar manner by 680 Squadron.

Night fighter operations were conducted from Malta in 1944 by 256 Squadron which flew defensive sorties over Naples, the Anzio beach-head and over Allied convoys using Mosquito Mks XII and XIII. By late 1944 256 Squadron was flying Ranger sorties into the Balkans. The last few weeks of 1944 saw the arrival of

Above left *Although Mosquitoes served for some highly secret experimental work their basic outline was almost unaltered at any time. MM308/G here, a PR Mk XVI, was fitted with American H2X Mickey radar for tests at Alconbury in early 1944 (de Havilland).*

Left *'Old Faithful', the first Australian-built Mosquito to go into action against the Japanese.*

Right *Engines roaring flat out and deeply, tail up, wet runway — all the thrill of a Mosquito getting away in a hurry. Mk XIII MM555 KP:B if you must know, taking off from Lille/Vendeville (R.H. Finlayson).*

Below right *MM560 a Mosquito NF XIII of 409 (RCAF) Squadron photographed at Le Culot on October 5 1944. AEAF stripes remain in evidence. As KP:F this aircraft destroyed four enemy aircraft whilst with 409 Squadron from June 1944 to February 1945 (R.H. Finlayson).*

the Mosquito XXX and XIX in Mediterranean Air Command, 255 and 600 Squadron receiving the latter type. The culmination of hostilities in the area brought no lessening in Mosquito activity. Indeed, in the immediate post-war period there came a greater diversity of Mosquito variants to that area than ever before.

One of the versions which saw post-war service in the Middle East was the PR Mk 34. It was developed as a result of attempts to much increase the range of the reconnaissance Mosquito for Far East service. Initially the hope was that 200 gallon drop tanks could merely be attached to the wings of the PR XVI, but the aircraft was insufficiently stressed to carry such a heavy outboard load. A revision of the PR XVI was made to permit the use of 200-gallon drop tanks, to which was added the swollen bomb bay so typical of the later bombers. Into it fuel tanks were placed so that a possible fuel tankage of 1,256 gallons could be carried.

The Far East, for which the PR 34 was intended, was the last zone of wartime RAF activity to be invaded by Mosquitoes. After limited deliveries in 1943, the apparent success of the wooden structure in none-too-suitable climatic conditions was such that, by January 1944, the plan was for 22 squadrons to fly Mosquitoes in the Far East on strike, reconnaissance, intruder and night fighter duties. To support them a repair facility was set up. The elaborate plan never came to fruition, there was never a need to employ so many aircraft.

Throughout 1944 684 Squadron, flying a mixture of Mk IXs and XVIs, carried out lengthy PR sorties to distant Siam (known as Thailand from 1949), the Nicobars and to Burma in a region that was as difficult to operate in as any. Long flights of over 2,000 miles were commonplace, sometimes in conditions of utmost severity. To increase the range of such missions PR 34s were employed after a scheme for an in-flight refuelled version of the PR XVI was dropped.

Although never so extensive as planned, the force of FB VIs was born in January 1944 when 1672 Conversion Unit began to train crews for 45 Squadron wherein Vengeances were replaced in February 1944. Training and operational work-up were slow and it was July 1944 before the second squadron, 82, was converted to Mosquitoes and October 1944 before 45 Squadron commenced operational flying with attacks on roads, railways and ferry boats.

On October 20 1944 a Mosquito of 45 Squadron was engaged on a practice bombing flight when, without the

slightest warning, it suffered structural failure. Heat and exposure had at last taken their toll; fabric cracked and skinning was torn off the spar. The answer was to use formaldehyde glue, but this meant that a considerable number of Mosquito VIs already in India could never be used. This trouble could not have come at a worse time, for operations to recapture Burma were about to begin and Mosquitoes were urgently needed for night interdictor flying.

New aircraft were rushed to 45 Squadron which resumed operations in November 1944 with 82 Squadron following suit the next month, by which time Mosquitoes were flying day and night interdictor missions and from time to time tangling with Japanese fighters.

The turn of the year found 47 Squadron converting followed by 84 and 110 Squadrons, as the build-up continued for a final assault on ex-British territory in the Far East. But the glue problem had interrupted conversion and delivery so that the intended sustained, regular campaign of day and night operations did not manifest itself. Instead, 45, 47 and 82 Squadrons found

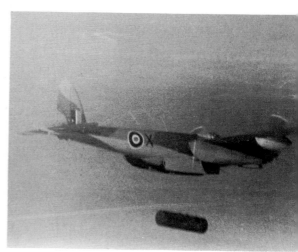

Above left *Particularly useful in the Far East were the later variants of the photographic Mosquitoes. Ground staff are seen here carrying one of the large film cameras, beneath a Mosquito PR XVI of 684 Squadron (IWM).*

Above right *Caught in the act, and a rare sight for sure. A Mosquito XVI of 128 Squadron drops its 'cookie'.*

Below *What a thrill to have walked along the production line for Mk XXs at Toronto, noting the shrouded exhausts and the canopy blisters and much else.*

Above far right *A group of Mosquito B XXVs awaiting delivery from Canada to Britain. Both KB660 and KB695 (foreground) were transferred to the Royal Navy in summer 1945.*

themselves engaged in Operation Dracula wherein they flew standing patrols allowing 'cab rank' style strikes during the battle for Rangoon. This took place at the time when 684 Squadron was facing tropical storms during very deep penetrations, and photographing the infamous Burma-Siam railway.

Slow expansion of the Mosquito force in the Far East during 1944-5 contrasted sharply with the highly efficient manner in which 8 Group was able to expand the LNSF and conduct an almost nightly bombing campaign on Germany. Not only was a force of around 120 Mosquitoes available for nightly operations, they could now deliver very heavy bomb tonnages since many were Mk XVI aircraft.

During 1944 the delivery of Mk XXs increased fast and in August 608 Squadron was reformed to operate them from Downham Market. 128 Squadron reformed in September 1944. The Mk XVI bombers were able to carry a 4,000 lb bomb during flights with an action radius of 600 miles. In October 1944 the first operational sorties by Mk XXVs were flown, this being the Canadian-built version of the B Mk IV fitted with Packard Merlin 225s.

By January 1945 the LNSF had a strength of eight squadrons for which 139 and 162 were now both carrying H2S radar in the noses of their aircraft which formed a special marker force for the Force's bombing operations. The other two marker squadrons, 105 and 109, continued very often to spearhead main force attacks with the aid of Oboe. The range of the latter was much extended when new, continental-based stations came into use.

On nearly every war-time night in 1945 Mosquitoes of 8 Group operated. A straining groan as, heavily laden, they circled base for high-level exit, was something one came to associate with the East Anglia of those days. The target? A fair guess always would be Berlin, that city which had so tantalisingly appealed to the Mosquito protagonists. In February 1945 Mosquito night bombers flew 2,404 sorties with a very high success rate and for only seven losses. On 13 nights Mosquitoes bombed Berlin, and their loads were hefty by any reckoning. The German capital was bombed on the first night when 91 Mosquitoes operated, on March 21/22 139 sorties were directed against the 'Big City'. Out of 2,950 sorties despatched in March 1945 only nine Mosquitoes failed to return, this being the peak month of Mosquito night bomber activity.

As spoof attackers, early Window droppers, a force able to mount a knock-out blow sometimes against a very small target, 8 Group's Mosquito force was without doubt the most accurate and tractable part of Bomber Command. At the start of April 1945 an average of around 200 Mosquitoes was daily available for operations, the serviceability rate being very high. Bomber Command's Mosquitoes ended their bombing war with attacks on airfields and targets around Kiel Bay.

It was in sea routes leading to that area that the final

shots from Coastal Command's Mosquitoes were fired. The effectiveness of the Beaufighter had continued to the end of hostilities. On balance the Beaufighter was probably more suitable for overseas theatres than the Mosquito and by 1944 many were serving away from Britain.

The second Coastal Command squadron to use Mosquitoes, 235 at Portreath, was not equipped until June 1944. By the end of that month both Coastal Command squadrons were operating, mainly in the south-west approaches and over Biscay. The capture of western France lessened the need for Coastal Command operations in that area, but the Germans still had to maintain links with their occupation forces in Norway and were continuing to ship iron ore from Narvik. Both Coastal Command squadrons therefore moved north to Banff, by Moray Firth, in September 1944 where they were joined by 333 (Norwegian) Squadron, and the Beaufighters in the area, for strike operations.

Against merchant ships, some quite small, the aerial torpedo was a costly weapon which did not always bring the desired result. Coastal Command was now in possession of a far more effective device, the unguided rocket projectile which was very effective when fired against soft-skinned armour and ships. In late September 248 Squadron commenced firing such rockets, four being carried beneath each mainplane. The absence of recoil was a great advantage. Both 25 lb solid head AP rockets and 60 lb SAP rockets were available and, in October 1948, 248 Squadron began to fire them during anti-shipping strikes.

In the month following, 143 Squadron started operating Mosquitoes and a period of exhilarating operations commenced. Coastal Command's war, long hours of patrol interspersed with brief periods of hectic action, was echoed in the Mosquito strikes. A long flight across the North Sea needing infinite care and skill would be made to avoid radar detection and fighter interception. Then would follow an attack often as alarming as it must, in retrospect anyway, have been both frightening and thrilling. Such attacks had often to be delivered against ships sheltering in narrow fjords, which meant very steep dive attack with anti-aircraft guns blazing away *across* the fjord. The risk of aerial collision or colliding with a mountainside was ever apparent and for the watchers on the ground the noise as bombs, rockets and gunfire mingled was hellish. Then, seemingly without warning would come the silence only a Norwegian fjord can offer. A Coastal Command drama would have been played out yet again.

In the first months of 1945 Coastal Command's Mosquitoes took an ever more important part in the anti-shipping war with 235 Squadron also firing rockets. April 1945 saw operations being even further stepped up particularly against the remaining U-boats. On April 9 alone three U-boats were sunk by Mosquitoes, not using the six-pounder gun of the Mk XVIII but more conventionally.

One of the most memorable operations of the period came on April 19 1945 when a mixture of rocket-firing and depth charge armed Mosquitoes of 143, 235, 248 and 333 Squadrons flying over the North Sea came upon a mixed force of 18 Ju 88s and Ju 188s the like of which must have seemed like a mirage or a throw back to years long past. The Mosquitoes slammed their ammunition into the enemy formation and sent nine bombers to a watery end.

As with Bomber Command, Coastal Command too was still increasing its Mosquito strength even as the European war was ending, 404 Squadron replacing its Beaufighters with Mosquito VIs and first operating them on April 22, then promptly using them to shoot down a Bv 138 flying-boat. In March 1945 248 Squadron had passed the handful of Mk XVIIIs to 254 Squadron who promply put them to good use against midget submarines. To the end of hostilities Coastal Command's Mosquitoes patrolled around the shores of Denmark during a period of activity which for the Command was one of its busiest and, indeed, most costly.

But of all the Mosquitoes at work in the closing stages of the war it was those of 2 Group that performed the most thrilling of operations. Much of the Group's use of the Mosquito remained at night, whenever the weather permitted it — and sometimes when it did not. The Mk VIs would pester the enemy from about 20 miles behind his forward positions to considerable distances into enemy territory. There was a hectic period before the Arnhem landings when attacks were made upon barracks. A raid on Aarhus University building, in Denmark, by 24 Mosquitoes on October 31 1944 once again came to grip public imagination as the Mk VI yet again proved to be a very accurate weapon to pit against an enemy outpost.

Until November 1944 the 2 Group Mosquitoes were sited in the south of England, but fast advance through France demanded some at least be moved forward and so the three squadrons of 138 Wing moved to Epinoy, leaving 140 Wing still at Thorney Island. Thick fog in December which permitted von Rundstedt's advance in the Ardennes grounded the Mk VIs. When they were able to resume operations they did so intensively so that two sorties per night were flown by many aircraft.

The fighter-bomber Mosquitoes were much involved

HP858 an FB Mk VI was an early Coastal Command Mosquito having been delivered to 10 MU on September 11 1943 and joining 333 (Norwegian) Squadron at Leuchars a week later. The Squadron specialised in reconnaissance flights along the Norwegian coast, and on January 21 1944 HP858 confronted a Bv 138 flying-boat which was shot down. At this time the aircraft was coded KK:K (in Sky) on its usual Dark Green-Medium Sea Grey finish. The squadron took the aircraft to Banff on September 30 1944 from where the squadron's Mosquitoes first acted as outriders for Coastal Command strikes off Norway and later fully participated in the strikes and dropped depth charges on to submarines. HP858 came to Cambridge for overhaul in the summer of 1945, by which time it was to be seen in the Extra Dark Sea Grey/Sky finish with black spinners and Sky codes depicted here. It flew to 51 MU Lichfield in September 1945 and was sold as scrap in June 1950.

Above *TW256, a Mosquito TR 33 showing a torpedo being carried. The Extra Dark Sea Grey/Sky aircraft has black spinners, numbers and codes. It was recorded in the hands of 771 Squadron at Lee-on-Solent in November 1948 having been delivered to the Royal Navy in mid-1946.*

Below *Mosquito B XX KB115 which saw post-war service at RAE Farnborough.*

against communication targets in February, these attacks coming to a climax with Operation Clarion, a daylight operation in which many Mosquitoes of 2 TAF took part. A month later came the next memorable low-level operation.

In the Shellhaus building in Copenhagen the Gestapo imprisoned and tortured Danish patriots. Bursting a wall to allow them to escape, as at Amiens, was a much more difficult task, but the building was attacked by 140 Wing on March 20 1945, 18 Mosquitoes taking part from their advanced base at Fersfield. Such operations were always hazardous in the extreme. This one was no exception. One aircraft collided with a mast and crashed on to a convent school. Some following crews mistook the burning wreckage for Shellhaus even though all possible care was being taken.

An intensive interdictor campaign was meanwhile being waged against German forces guarding the Rhine, and in the sector immediately behind the front line. During the period of the Rhine crossing 2 Group gave very close support, pestering the enemy at night to the end of hostilities. One other low-level attack came on April 17 on a target in Odense. But such operations pale into insignificance when compared with 2 Group's night offensive. During post-war interrogation many Wehrmacht officers and men related how the continuous nightly operations wore the army down, for the Mosquito sting prevented any rest and lowered morale.

The end of the war in Europe meant that a sustained attempt could now be made to bring the Far East war to a successful conclusion. By May 1945 the long-range Mosquito PR 34 was a going concern and in June this variant entered service with a detachment of 684 Squadron based on the Cocos Islands. RG185:Z was, on July 3 1945, the first of its type to operate. The Mk 34's

range possibilities made very long duration flights possible, the longest being of nine hours five minutes and it was flown to Penang and Taiping.

Also delivered to the Far East was the Mk XIX for a possible night intruder campaign. 89 Squadron received this variant in July 1945, then 176 Squadron equipped, but there were no operations using this version.

Build-up of the Mosquito VI squadrons in the Far East continued, 211 Squadron equipping in June 1945, for it seemed likely that more Mosquito VIs would be needed for a possible assault on Singapore.

With the Mosquito strength in the Far East ever increasing now that the gluing problem had been overcome, and the needs in Europe lessened,

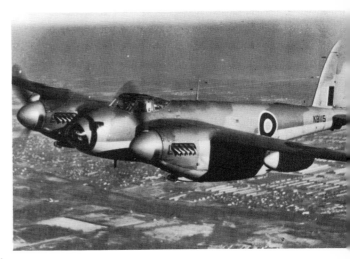

Mosquitoes were being hurried east so that a large number were in India when the war ended.

One of the first post-war tasks Mosquitoes undertook was a photo survey of Indo-China, and then one of Cambodia flown from Bangkok. Operations against Japanese forces in Indonesia were no sooner over than they had to be resumed, this time against Indonesians intent upon driving out any Dutchmen wishing to resume occupation of the land. 82, 84 and 110 Squadrons all participated in attacks on guerilla forces, making use of rockets for the first time in the Far East during their attacks. Not until March 12 1946 did Mosquitoes of 47 Squadron fire the concluding rounds. This, though, was far from the end of an operational role for Mosquitoes in the Far East.

In Europe 2 Group's Mosquito squadrons remained as part of the British Air Forces of Occupation in Germany. Squadrons relied upon the Mk VI or the B Mk 35, an up-dated version of the B XVI loosely based upon the PR 34. Thus, it was possible to convert a few Mk 35s quite easily into PR aircraft for specialised roles. The VIs and 35s changed squadron numbers in the post-war wind-down and re-adjustment, soldiering on until 2 TAF took delivery of Vampires.

In Britain the Mosquito squadrons of 8 Group soon were disbanded until only 109 and 139 remained keeping their marker role and specialising in the use of Gee-H until the coming of the Canberra in 1952. Six Mosquito night fighter squadrons were held, on half strength, until 1954. At the end of the war they had been flying Mk XXXs but in 1946-7 Mk 36s replaced them. Different radar and engines distinguished this refinement of the Mk XXX which also served in small numbers for night defence of the Egyptian Canal Zone until the mid-1950s when Meteor night fighters or Vampire NF 10s took over.

Coastal Command rapidly relinquished the use of Mosquitoes after the war. The maritime strike role was much under discussion, and in a period when the only possible foe was not very naval-orientated there was little need for a strike force. The end of the Mosquito as a maritime aircraft though was far from on hand.

In 1943 thought had been directed to the Royal Navy operating Mosquitoes from carriers. There was some doubt about the strength of the fuselage, and the aircraft's general suitability for operations at sea. After study there seemed no sound reasons militating against Mosquito carrier operations. A prototype was produced, with folding wings and arrester hook. Provision was made for bombs or rockets under the mainplanes and a torpedo under the belly which, incidentally, some of the bombers could also have carried. This naval version became the TR Mk 33 and in revised form the TR 37. Intervening Marks in the 20s had been allocated to variants to be built in Canada. Mark numbers in the 30s were for British designs, leaving the 40s for Australian production. Like many Canadian examples, the Australian Mosquitoes saw limited post-war service and similarly ranged through

Above left *Plenty of detail, ideal for model making, is shown in this photograph of a Mosquito TR 33, photographed at the Heston display of October 2 1945.*

Left *A stage in the development of a navalised Mosquito was the modification of FB Mk VI LR359 whose under surfaces were yellow and upper surfaces the usual naval grey and green shades. Note the four-bladed propellers.*

Below left *A close-up of the deck arrestor hook on LR359. The lower sections of the 'P' marking are merely black outline. After stress tests at Farnborough from November 1943 the aircraft carried out deck landing trials on HMS Indefatigable from Renfrew until it was destroyed in a flying accident at Arbroath on November 9 1944 (de Havilland).*

Above *The fully navalised TR Mk 33 became available in 1945. Its wing folding feature is shown here in the photograph of June 1945 (de Havilland).*

Below *'Trolley-acc' still plugged in, engines running and all set for action. A silver finished PR XVI of 684 Squadron in the Far East (IWM).*

variants with single and two-stage supercharged engines.

The Royal Navy took delivery of 100 Mk 33s, and sundry other Mosquitoes, and placed them into 811 Squadron based at Ford and Brawdy and five non-operational squadrons. As with the Coastal Command Mk VIs, these naval Mosquitoes arrived as the navy was winding down and tactical requirements were making conventional torpedo attack an outdated system.

Another use for naval Mosquitoes was as target aircraft or for target towing. A need to photograph the results of predicted fire against aerial targets led to the development of a most grotesque Mosquito, the TT Mk 39 with a huge glazed nose comprising a great number of optically flat panels. Only a handful of such aircraft were produced by converting Mk XVIs, and were used mainly for training in the Mediterranean area.

Perhaps it was logical that it should be in the Far East where the Mosquitoes arrived last, that their final operations should take place. The Turks, the Belgians, Swedes, Yugoslavs, Czechs, Chinese, Israelis, Norwegians, Dominican Republic and the French all acquired surplus Mosquitoes. The French made good use of them during their sorry campaign in Indo-China. Between January 1947 and July 1949 Mosquito VIs were used as strike aircraft against Communist forces. And it was against similar unpleasant folk that the Mosquito last saw action.

When it was necessary to snuff out Communist insurrection in Malaya only 81 Squadron retained any Mosquitoes. Their PR 34s went into action in July 1949 securing photographs of all areas where the terrorists might be hiding and subsequently keeping watch for any signs of their whereabouts. Only half of the squadron flew Mosquitoes, the remainder used Spitfire XIXs. For nearly seven years jungle photography was a daily task for 81 Squadron's Mosquitoes until December 15 1955. By then the aircraft were badly worn, and the jet age had blossomed. It fell to RG314 to make the last operational Mosquito sortie.

In Britain the final flights in RAF hands were far less glamorous. Training command still had a few T Mk IIIs, one of which has survived to be the last flying example of its type in Britain. Some Mk 35 bombers were converted into high-speed target tugs, mainly for anti-aircraft co-operation work, doubling up sometimes as target aicraft. It surely is a measure of the success of the Mosquito that it was able to perform such a task in a world of jet fighters.

The Mosquito's epitaph may well be seen in subsequent RAF bombers. As the war ended plans were being drawn up for a variety of jet bombers, the most successful of which, to Specification B.3/45, would be the Canberra. Not, let it be noted, a bomber armed with guns for self-defence but certainly a bomber with fighter speed.

Plans were about to be laid for long-range bombers able to carry nuclear stores, the most successful of which would be the Avro Vulcan. Once again, not a bomber armed with guns for self-defence but certainly a bomber with fighter speed.

The lesson had been learnt, but probably too late.

Below *Of the Australian PR Mk 41 28 examples (A52-300-37) were built and delivered between May 1947 and July 1948. The Mk 41 was a post-war updated version of the Mk 40.*

Above right *An interim post-war colour scheme for reconnaissance Mosquitoes is visible here. Whilst RG210:V of 684 Squadron remains silver over-all another PR 34 RG263 close at hand has PR Blue undersurfaces and spinners. Note the paddle-bladed propellers.*

Right *Only limited use of the Mosquito was made by the Royal Navy. A production TR Mk 33 TW256 is seen here.*

Below right *Disposal of many of the Mosquitoes remaining in Canada was partly to Nationalist China in whose hands B-M016 an FB Mk 26, may be seen. The finish was dark green and light grey.*

Left *A later stage in post-war PR Mosquito markings is shown by another PR 34 PF662 which has the post-war 'D' Type fuselage roundel. Note, too, the forward facing camera in the wing drop tank, and 540 Squadron's badge on the fin.*

Below left *Much more refined in the target towing role was the TT 35 with winch and drogue equipment beneath the fuselage and towing cable deflecting equipment on the tailplane. Colouring was silver with black and yellow stripes on the underside.*

Below *In the British Air Forces of Occupation in Germany FB Mk VIs were supplemented by B Mk 35s like these examples of 98 Squadron (M.J. Smith).*

Above right *After the war the French made use of Mosquitoes in Africa and Indo-China as well as in Metropolitan France. RF995, a PR XVI, passed to the French in June 1946 after service with the Air Transport Trials and Development Unit (E.C. Armées).*

Right *In Britain night fighter squadrons used the NF 36 into the 1950s, and usually had a T Mk 3 on hand for flying training. Silver/yellow VA893 Q:RO belongs to 29 Squadron (J.D.R. Rawlings).*

Below right *Mosquitoes proved extremely useful after the end of hostilities for a number of major surveys needed at home and overseas, this occupying the Benson squadrons for many years. DH:A — PF679, PR Blue over-all and photographed at Northolt on September 25 1948, served at this time.*

Above far left *A B Mk 35 TH998 in post-war Bomber Command Medium Sea Grey—Black finish. This aircraft, wearing a Red serial, was used for photographic purposes during de Havilland's guided weapons development programme in 1953.*

Above left *In the Middle East Mosquitoes performed post-war in a mixture of roles, and in RAF and naval hands. T Mk III RR296 RT:N was used at Fayid in 1947 (B.T. Gibbins).*

Left *The only ugly Mosquito, the TT 39 with optically flat nose panels for photography of gunnery results. The TT 39 was a conversion of the B XVI. PF606 is depicted (David Menard).*

Below left *Relatively few Mosquitoes survived intact beyond the 1950s. One of the late survivors has been this B Mk 35 TA639 in something akin to its day bomber RAF finish (J.D.R. Rawlings).*

Above *Only two Mosquitoes remain airworthy in Britain. One is the all-silver B 35 at Strathallan, the other British Aerospace's T Mk III RR299.*

What effect crew reductions and high-level operations within and by Bomber Command during the war would have had on its outcome is a matter for surmise. It is reasonable to suggest that losses in men, materials and training needs would have, to say the least, been different. It is easy to be wise after the event.

Only when the jet bombers and fighters became available was the Mosquito retired from front line service. Fourteen years of such service is not a record, but no other aircraft in the history of military flying has served in such a wide range of roles.

After a story of phenomenal success a strange aspect remains. In respect of their public image the Spitfire, the Hurricane and the Lancaster still win tremendous popular support. Great crowds fall silent as the last of their breed scurry by, and it is good that they should. Bring on a Mosquito and the reception is less intense. This is partly due to the exceptional secrecy that surrounded the Mosquito for much of its war. Its operations were secret, as was its radar and also its manner of employment. No pre-war high-speed run

from Edinburgh to Northolt as the Hurricane made. No Battle of Britain to fight and win. No courageous low-level race to Augsburg which brought the Lancaster into the public eye almost at the start of its career.

Instead, high-level lone sorties which, it was hoped, the enemy was as ignorant of as the British public. Low-level raids to places of great secrecy, and hush-hush operations cloaked in darkness. Many months passed before it was admitted that the Mosquito existed and by the end of the war the terse words, 'Last night Mosquitoes bombed Berlin without loss to themselves . . .' was about the limit of most public awareness of what the Mosquito had achieved. In folk lore, this superb, nay stupendous aeroplane, the most cost-effective warplane of all time, is unlikely ever to take its rightful place.

What now is important is that the Mosquito is known to have achieved everything, and more, and that it did it better than any other aircraft. The combination of the world's finest aircraft, in the hands of the world's finest air force was unbeatable.

Chapter Six

Preserved Mosquitoes
by Stuart Howe

During the war, the Mosquito could take a tremendous amount of punishment and still keep flying, but how did this classic aeroplane stand up to the passage of time, and just how many have survived the 35 years since the war's end? Well, fortunately, as you will see from this chapter a surprising number do still exist, partly due to the fact that a few examples were still in service up until 1963, when the preservation movement was just starting to take hold. But in many cases it was due to the Mosquito's very construction — the scrap metal merchants were not interested in wooden aeroplanes, so a number were bought by farmers and other interested parties or just lay derelict until rescued by the growing band of enthusiasts. Let's, then, take a look at the survivors of this remarkable aeroplane.

Australia
Kogarah, NSW

Here at The Camden Museum of Aviation, ex-DHA employee G. H. Thomas stores FB VI HR621. I have no accurate report as to her present condition, but she is believed to need restoration. HR621 was constructed by Standard Motors, Coventry, in late 1944 and was despatched by sea to Australia in December 1944. Her subsequent history is unknown, and details plus photos would be appreciated.

Lidcombe, Sydney

There is a third Mosquito, Australian-built PR Mk 40 A52-210. Built at Bankstown late in 1944 she was modified to become a PR 41 and re-numbered A52-319. She did not see any service life, and was eventually sold to Captain J. Woods of Perth WA in March 1953 who put the aircraft on the civilian register as VH-WAD. Plans to fly her fell through and she sat at Perth airport on display, slowly deteriorating. Subsequently she was bought by American David Kubista, but before he could get her out of the country she was badly vandalised, her back broken and in very poor condition, and lay at Sydney docks for several years. She has subsequently been bought for $21,000 by the Australian War Memorial Museum and is being restored by Hawker de Havilland Australia Pty Ltd first-year apprentices at Lidcombe, Sydney. Two to three years is the estimate for completion of the restoration.

Mildura, Victoria

The 'Warbirds' Aviation Museum at Mildura airport has in its collection the only surviving PR XVI, NS631. This machine arrived in Australia in November 1944 when she was re-numbered A52-600. Issued to 87 PRU Squadron, she did some 20 missions over enemy territory, ranging from 6 hours to 15½ hours duration. Then used by 5 Squadron and AGRS. After conversion to an instructional airframe on October 22 1947, NS631 was disposed of in November 1954 with 321½ hours total time to her credit. After 12 years outside she was bought by Pearce Dunn for his museum. The wings were sawn off, but Pearce has all the parts and her restoration is progressing slowly.

Belgium
Brussels

At the *Musée de L'Armée* is the unique NF 30, RK952. Leavesden-built early in 1945, RK952 did not see operational RAF service, but was delivered to Belgium in October 1951 becoming MB24. She saw service with the 10th Belgian Wing, coded ND:N, ending her service career in October 1956 at Bauvechain, the following year moving to the Brussels museum. She was re-painted in 1968 with her Belgian serial MB24, and is today one of the Museum's star attractions. She is in excellent condition.

Canada
Calgary, Alberta

At the airport the Centennial Planetarium holds a number of aircraft, including B 35 RS700. Airspeed built she was taken on charge by the RAF in February 1946, and then went to several Maintenance Units, until converted to PR 35 standards in 1952, eventually being sold in December 1954 and used for two years by 5 Squadron. She became CF-HMS to the Canadian survey company, Spartan Airways. Several years ago there were plans to restore RS700 to airworthy condition, but these seem to have fallen through and she has since remained in store. Present plans are unknown, and up to-date information would be appreciated.

Edmonton, Alberta

On the outskirts of this city, another ex-Spartan machine VP189/CF:HMQ is being restored. After being used by Spartan until 1966, she was displayed on the

by Standard Motors in October 1945, TE910 did not see operational service, and was earmarked for delivery to the RNZAF. She departed from Pershore in March 1947 being flown via India, arriving on April 3 1947, when she was taken on charge at Ohakea for use by 75 Squadron, coded YC:B. She was declared surplus in June 1955 and sold to enthusiast John Smith. The Mosquito is complete, and until John can put up a permanent building, he has erected a temporary roof over his aircraft to keep out the weather.

South Africa

Johannesburg

In the South African National Museum of Military History at Saxonwold is displayed PR IX, LR480. Hatfield-built in the second half of 1943 she was soon flown to the Middle East. On June 8 1944 she was issued to 60 Squadron stationed at Foggia in Italy, and saw service over the Balkans and Austria. On August 25 new engines were fitted, and in December Colonel O. G. Davies set out to break the speed record from Cairo to Pretoria in LR480, but damaged the aircraft's under-carriage during an unscheduled landing on a 700-yard strip at Que-Que in Southern Rhodesia. The aircraft was repaired at Gwelo and flown to South Africa and, in 1946, was donated by the SAAF to the Museum, after a total flying time of 216 hours. LR480 is in excellent shape and is much admired by all.

USA

Chino, California

Here in flyable condition with Yesterday's Air Force is TT 35 RS709. Built as a B 35 at Christchurch early in 1946 she was stored at 15 MU Wroughton until May 1952 when she was flown to Brooklands Aviation at Sywell for conversion to target tug standards. After the mods were completed she was delivered to 236 OCU (used from September 1952 to September 1954) and then, for a time, into store with 27 MU at Shawbury and thence onto Civilian Anti-Aircraft Co-operation Unit at Exeter, coded 47 on June 7 1956. She remained at Exeter until May 1963 when she was declared surplus and was sold on July 11 to the Mirisch Film Company as G-AKSA for use in the now classic film *633 Squadron* as HT:B. After filming she was bought by Peter Thomas of the Skyfame Aircraft Museum at Staverton. In 1971 she was bought by Ed Jurist of New York who based her with the Confederate Air Force at Harlingen in Texas. Due to a sick engine she did not fly while in Texas and was again sold and was duly delivered to her present owner at Chino. (Stop press: I have just discovered that she has recently been purchased by Doug Arnold for his collection at Blackbush.)

Placentia, California

In a somewhat sorry state here is FB VI PZ474, in the hands of James Merizan. This Mosquito has had an interesting, but not very exciting career, and is much travelled. She was built at Hatfield and was assigned to 19 MU at St Athan on April 19 1945. After use with 80 and 132 Operational Conversion Units (as GY-AR) she was sent to 51 MU in February 1946. She was then sold to New Zealand, arriving on April 15 1948, when she was given her new serial of NZ2384. This aircraft then saw very little service and was put into store until 1953 when she, and several others, were purchased for export by Aircraft Supplies (NZ) Ltd, and given the civil registration of ZK-BCV. After she was flown out to America in February 1955, the government stepped in and prevented the departure of the others, so rumour has it, because the aircraft were destined for use as military machines in a South American country. On arrival in the US ZK-BCV was put on the American register as N9909F, owned by the Insurance Finance Corporation of Studio City, California. Here she stayed for many years and was cancelled from the civil register in December 1970. After being 'stored' outside for three years (during which time some kind person had sawn the fuselage in half!), it was purchased by US Navy pilot James Merizan. The aircraft, especially the fuselage, is in poor condition and Jim was considering the possible use of plastics in an effort to restore her, when I last heard from him.

Silver Hill, Maryland

Here, at the National Air and Space Museum's store and restoration facility is B 35 TH998, still dismantled but in good condition. Delivered from Hatfield to storage at Shawbury in August 1945, she did not fly again until 1952 when she was flown to Brooklands for TT conversion, joining 3 CAACU in September. Declared surplus in 1962 she was presented to the NASM in August 1963, where she has remained ever since. With some 200 or so airframes to restore it is unlikely that the NASM will get around to TH998 for some considerable time. The USAF Museum at Dayton are anxious to obtain a Mosquito for display, so perhaps one day soon it would be possible to transfer her to this museum?

The information contained in this chapter is somewhat sparse in places, especially concerning the Mosquitoes preserved abroad, so I would be most grateful for any additional information, corrections and photographs which could be included in a future edition of this book. Thank you.

Any information?

With the Confederate Air Force at Harlington, Texas, are the remains of a Mosquito (could be RG300) consisting of engine nacelles, canopy, tailplane and radiators. History, please?

T III RR299 going through its air show routine at a Shuttleworth Collection display in July 1977.

A summary of preserved Mosquitoes

Mark No	Serial	Country	Location	Remarks
Prototype	W4050	GB	London Colney, Hertfordshire	Displayed
NF II	HJ711	GB	York	Re-building
T III	RR299	GB	Hawarden, Cheshire	Airworthy
T III	TV959	GB	London	Displayed
T III	TW117	GB	London	Displayed
FB VI	HR621	Australia	Kogarth, NSW	Stored
FB VI	PZ474	USA	Placentia, California	Re-building
FB VI	TA122	GB	London Colney, Hertfordshire	Displayed (fuselage only)
FB VI	TE758	NZ	Christchurch	Stored
FB VI	TE863	NZ	Christchurch	Stored
FB VI	TE910	NZ	Nelson, South Island	Stored
PR IX	LR480	SA	Johannesburg	Displayed
PR XVI	NS631	Australia	Mildura, Victoria	Stored
B 20	KB336	Canada	Rockcliffe, Ontario	Displayed
FB 26	KA114	Canada	Richmond, BC	Stored
NF 30	RK952	Belgium	Brussels	Displayed
B 35	RS700	Canada	Calgary, Alberta	Stored
B 35	RS709	USA	Chino, California	TT35 Airworthy
B 35	RS712	GB	Auchterarder, Scotland	TT35 Airworthy
B 35	TA634	GB	London Colney, Hertfordshire	TT35 Displayed
B 35	TA639	GB	Cosford, Shropshire	TT35 Displayed
B 35	TA719	GB	Duxford, Cambridgeshire	TT35 Displayed
B 35	TH988	USA	Silver Hill, Maryland	Stored
B 35	TJ118	GB	London Colney/Oxford	Re-building, TT35 (fuselage only)
B 35	TJ138	GB	Swinderby, Yorkshire	TT35 Stored
B 35	VP189	Canada	Edmonton, Alberta	Re-building
B 35	VR796	Canada	Kapuskasing, Ontario	Re-building
B 35	TA717	Canada	Mission, BC	Re-building
PR 41	A52-210	Australia	Lidcombe, Sydney	Re-building
FB 40	A52-19	NZ	Ardmore, Auckland	Re-building

I have listed each aircraft by its original serial number, which is not necessarily its subsequent or current serial number.

Chapter Seven

Basic materials

The development and exploits of the Mosquito recounted in the first part of this book, and the imaginary operations created by Frederick E. Smith in his books about the fictional 633 Squadron, would appear to provide adequate incentive for kit manufacturers to have flooded the market with kits of the 'wooden wonder' as they have done with other legendary aircraft. The pocket-money modeller who revels in the play value of his creations, must surely have just as much material available to him to venture into his land of make-believe with a Mosquito as he does with the endless offerings of Spitfires, Thunderbolts, Bf 109s and FW 190s. However, this type of modeller, and the one who 'builds-a-kit-a-day' must not be deprecated, as it is their money which provides the mass market so essential if the serious modeller is to benefit by the release of just as important but less commercially viable models. Even at the longest stretch of the imagination the Mosquito cannot be placed into the latter category, and in recent years the balance has been somewhat redressed by the release of two splendid 1:72 kits and a 1:48 scale offering. Prior to this there was only the early 1:72 scale kit (No 02001-9) in the Airfix series 2, and a somewhat dated 1:48 scale model (No PA 129-200) from Monogram supported by a 1:32 scale model from Revell.

In this chapter it is proposed to look at the kits avail-

able at the time of writing and discuss their various merits; there seems little point, however, in including the above-mentioned Airfix kit as it was a very early release and although with a lot of work it could be made into a fairly decent model, it has long been superseded by a much better kit from the same manufacturer. If you are a collector of kits it might be worthwhile looking for this Airfix offering either as a singleton or part of the Dogfight Double kit when it shared a box with a Messerschmitt Me 262. Another kit which is now hard to find is the Frog 1:72 scale (No F187), but this one will be included in the following evaluation since it has some useful components — that is if you are prepared to cannibalise what some consider to be a collector's item.

Apart from some late Marks produced for target towing, and the odd experimental machine, the basic outline shape of the Mosquito remained virtually unchanged. This makes the task of converting to various Marks a not-too-difficult one, and certainly not beyond the skills of those who have only recently taken up this part of the hobby. In the space available it would clearly not be possible to cover every Mosquito variant, but those I have chosen include a wide enough selection to enable the basic guide lines for all conversions to be followed. I have steered clear of some of the more exotic variants and those used in experiments; in the latter category it would be possible to include those aircraft fitted with a

An NF 36 of 85 Squadron RAF. It is Dark Green/Medium Sea Grey with red codes and serials.

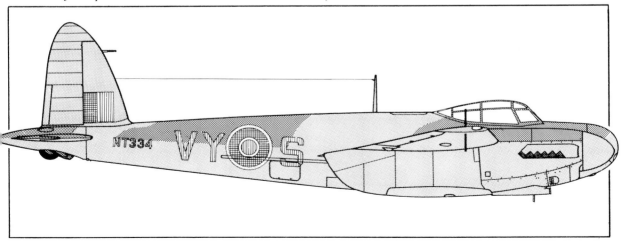

Bristol turret aft of the cockpit, but I felt that to achieve the main objective of this part of the book there was little scope for such one-off aircraft. The modeller who disagrees and perhaps specialises in the unusual is, I suspect, in the minority and will be quite capable of producing what he wants from the mass of material available on the Mosquito.

In my book *Making Model Aircraft* (Patrick Stephens Ltd, 1976) I made the point that any form of modelling is a very personal thing, and at the end of the day the result is usually only vitally important to the builder. If the pleasure the builder obtains from creating the best model of which he is capable satisfies him, then the object of the exercise has been achieved. I make no apologies for repeating my thoughts here and in so doing, stress that any methods I describe, materials used, and objectives obtained, are purely my own and I totally accept that there are many equally good and perhaps better ways of producing a variety of Mosquitoes.

In some cases I have not cross-kitted where clearly it would have been possible to do so. This is deliberate as I believe that it is not only good to practise skills in using wood or building in other materials, but wise to bear in mind that not every reader is able to buy three or four different kits to produce just two models. Quite clearly it would now be possible to produce every Mosquito ever built from the 1:72 scale kits on the market by exchanging components, equally it would be possible to

achieve the same goal from any one manufacturer's kit; the challenge rests with the individual and if I have been able to give some guidance then I shall feel I have succeeded.

The kits on the market as I write (early in 1979) vary from the old Airfix 1:72 model to the latest products. All my remarks apply to the kits as they are *now*. This is quite an important fact to keep in mind since manufacturers have a habit of changing box art and decals and the unsuspecting purchaser can find that what he thinks is — and indeed is sometimes advertised as — a new kit is only an old one slightly re-worked.

The production of any plastic kit is a costly exercise and quite often to keep tooling costs within acceptable proportions, bearing in mind that the final cost of the kit to the consumer must be reasonable, short cuts must be taken at the expense of some of the more subtle lines of the original. My own feelings are that such limitations must be accepted by the modeller and appreciated by the reviewer; but having made that clear I should also like to comment that there are really no excuses for serious errors in dimensions and outline shape where to produce the correct tool would cost no more than an incorrect one. A very good example is the completely incorrect shape of the fin/rudder in the Frog kit and the grossly oversize dimensions of the same component in the Monogram 1:48 scale model. I think it is essential that modellers, reviewers and writers try to keep a sense of proportion tempered with reality and in my comments

Below left *The throttle control box from an FB VI (Stuart Howe).*

Below right *The entry door from an FB VI; the notice states, 'Wind in trailing aerial before opening bomb door' (Stuart Howe).*

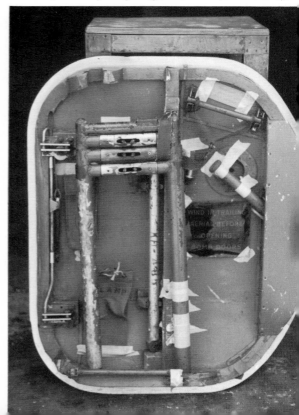

Right *The fuselage of an ex-4 Squadron FB VI arriving at Salisbury Hall. The tailwheel oleo and bulkhead as well as the fuselage strengthening strip are all clearly visible* (Stuart Howe).

Below right *Another useful shot of the 4 Squadron FB VI fuselage undergoing restoration. The bulged canopy windows are of interest as is the exact position and size of the fuselage strengthening strip* (Stuart Howe).

throughout this book I shall try to do this and will no doubt attract the attentions of those who, in many cases are self-appointed experts, and whose comments are true but impractical. There is absolutely no excuse for any competent modeller to produce an inaccurate model, the crucial issue is, where does one draw the line? If two modellers assemble, say, the Frog kit, and one corrects the offending fin/rudder whilst the other does not, when both are compared it is obvious that one is not a true representation of the outline shape of a Mosquito. Similarly, if the model with the incorrect shape is looked at in isolation even the tyro will know that there is something wrong, so obvious errors such as this must be corrected. But if one views the Matchbox kit made from the box without any alterations, how many will immediately recognise that the strengthening strake on the starboard side is too long?

In the latter example correction, as we shall see, is very easy, but the point I want to make is that if the kit error is of a minor nature it is doubtful if many will know it exists. I cannot see any point in adding 3 mm of plastic card, balsa or other material, to a fuselage length simply because someone says that it is that much too short. The work involved is not worth it and in lots of cases the saw cut necessary in cutting the offending fuselage in two will only increase the error and be completely forgotten when the modeller inserts his new material. Obviously as scale increases so too does the magnitude of dimensional error; if it is found that a 1:32 scale kit is a scale 50 cm short then it is well worth considering the insertion of this. It is all a question of keeping things in proportion. Although I have not wanted to give the impression of labouring these points, I may have done so both here and in other publications, but I do feel very strongly that too much store is placed in dimensional perfection when the capture of the correct outline and, perhaps most important of all, the 'feel' of the aircraft is of greater importance. Having made that point quite clear, I should also point out that I propose to mention such dimensional inaccuracies as I come across them, but it is entirely up to the reader as to how and whey he corrects them. The final comment on this aspect of modelling in general is worth quoting, as it was made to me by an employee of one of the major aircraft manufacturers who was helping with research into one of his company's aircraft; on showing some surprise about the length shown on one of the drawings I was told, 'What you must remember is that there are many criteria affecting the quoted over-all length. People often don't know if they are talking about the ground length, flight line length, lofting length and so

on, they also tend to forget that there are tolerances and it is doubtful if any two mass-produced aircraft have identical lengths. The proportions we are talking about in relation to the over-all airframe are very small, none the less they do exist and it would really be impossible to reproduce them in the scale you are speaking of'. Thus spoke a highly qualified aeronautical engineer and although it is taking things to extremes to use this quote in the context under discussion, it does make a very worthwhile point which is worth pondering over.

Since it seems that 1:72 scale is still the most popular among modellers let us first take a look at the kits of the Mosquito which are available in this size.

Airfix kit No 02009-1

This is the earliest kit of the Mosquito still available and the one mentioned earlier. Originally it was in this manufacturer's bagged series but was then marketed in a box in series two and has recently (March 1979) appeared in a new box. It is not really worth serious consideration but look out for the smart new box which shows aircraft EG:T and do not be fooled by it; the contents will still be the rather crude offering from very early moulds. If you are a keen collector then you will no doubt already have it or want to buy it, but the serious modeller will find a use only for the decals which

A good subject for diorama enthusiasts as an FB VI undergoes engine tests at the Standard Motor Co works (Roger Clinkscales).

are for an FB VI of 487 (RNZAF) Squadron. This kit also features in the series three Dogfight Double package from Airfix where it is numbered 03142-2.

Airfix kit No 03019-3

Released in 1973, this is still the finest 1:72 scale kit of the Mosquito and includes optional parts to make a Mk II (Special Intruder) of 23 Squadron RAF, a Mk VI fighter-bomber of 1 Squadron RAAF, and a Mk XVIII fighter-bomber of 248/254 Squadron RAF. All three versions have the single-stage Merlin engines without chin radiators, solid noses, and flat windscreen fighter canopies, so conversion to bomber and later marks requires cross-kitting with the Matchbox kit and/or some scratch-building.

This kit is very accurate in outline and the attention to detail cannot be faulted especially as no attempt has been made to compromise by using parts for one model which are 'nearly' right for another. The impression gained when first opening the box is that the model is complicated; this is not so and it is best to decide quite early on which particular version you propose to make, then sort out the parts accordingly, consigning the rest to the spares box where they will become extremely useful, especially if further Mosquitoes are to be built. Alternative parts included are: paddle blade propellers

for the Mk VI, a choice of shrouded or individual exhaust stacks, and alternative nose cones. The nose for the Mk II must be drilled to accept the 'bow and arrow' radar which is not fitted to the Mk VI, and the correct undertray (part 17) is used with either of these versions. For the Mk XVIII, which was fitted with a 57 mm Molins gun, the fuselage halves have to be cut along a pre-scribed line. This line is in fact the break-line on the original for alternative noses so it serves as a useful guide when it comes to conversions of either the clear-nosed bombers or radar-equipped — either 'thimble' or Universal-nosed — night fighters. The individual exhaust stacks are particularly useful items to have in the spares box but great care must be taken when carrying out conversion where the exhausts are exposed, as even a casual study of photographs will show some aircraft with six stacks and others with five, those in the kit are the five-stack variety. One very pleasing part of this kit is the Marstrand anti-shimmy tailwheel which is very nicely reproduced and adds that little touch of detail which can so easily be overlooked.

Although the fighter-style canopy is good and has delicate framing, the tooling has required a somewhat curved interior to facilitate removal from the mould, and this does cause a less than clear optical effect through the very sharp outside corners. This is only a

70

minor point which the purist might want to correct and the simple answer for those who have the equipment, is to use the kit canopy as a master from which to vac-form a new supply. The Mattel vac-form tool is ideal for this if you are lucky enough to have one or know a modeller who does.

Another area worth commenting on is the rear of the engine nacelles and the top surface of the wings where these meet. This area suffers from oversized rivets which should be either removed or at the very least rubbed down so that they are not as evident; as they stand in the kit they look like fugitives from Clydeside and tend to mar what is a very good model. My own personal preference is for practically complete removal since, if a full-size Mosquito is viewed from the distance where it appears to be 1:72 scale, the rivets would not be seen.

The cockpit interior consists of a bulkhead (part 9), a floor (part 7) two seats (parts 4 and 6), control column (part 8) and radio equipment (part 1). The seats are very rudimentary and should be replaced by scratch-built ones made from .010 plastic card, but if you do not want to tackle this then they can be improved by using the same material to add sides and a seat pan. The control column is the single type used on fighter versions and must be replaced by a yoke type when bomber conversions are made. Similarly the kit provides only the side entry door common to the fighter/fighter-bomber, whereas access to the cockpit in bomber Mosquitoes was through a floor hatch. Such points as this will be mentioned when it comes to conversions. There is no decal provided in the kit for an instrument panel so one must be either painted on to part 9 or made separately from paper or .005 plastic card and inserted during assembly. There are minor variations to all aircrafts' cockpit interiors and instrument panels but in this scale they would be more-or-less impossible to detect, so the general layout shown in drawings and photographs can be used.

There can be no doubt that the undercarriage assembly of this kit is the most accurate it would be possible to achieve in 1:72 scale. The oleo legs include the wheel door guides and fine locating pins for the mudguards which, although due to moulding requirements are slightly too thick, are very true to scale in shape. The wheels have the solid plain centre discs but the alternative drilled-out variety can be produced either by very careful manipulation of a fine drill or using wheel hubs from another kit. Soon after this kit was released I was discussing it with the late Bob Jones, who had a particular feeling for the Mosquito, and he told me that he proposed to use the wheel hubs from an Airfix Blenheim trimmed to fit the drilled-out centres of the Mosquito wheels. Having tried this I can confirm that it does work and looks most effective.

Close scrutiny of this kit seems to show that the taper on the under fuselage towards the tail is perhaps slightly inaccurate, but this does not detract in any way from the completed model and is, in my view, not worth correcting.

Above *A very useful view of the FB VI at Salisbury Hall clearly illustrating the wing root, entry door, nose compartment and canopy. This shot underlines how inaccurate the original Frog kit was as far as the distance between the wing root and lower line of the cockpit is concerned (Stuart Howe).*

Below and bottom *Post-war photographs of 4 Squadron's FB VIs showing a variety of camouflage styles, colours and markings. An aircraft from this unit is covered by Modeldecal sheet No 17 (Flight).*

Group Captain P.C. Pickard who led the famous raid against Amiens Prison during which he lost his life, walks in front of a Mk VI of 464 RAAF Squadron (W.A. Gray via Stuart Howe).

In addition to the alternative main airframe components, there are also optional external stores and these have the same fidelity of detail as the rest of the kit. The Mk XVIII can be fitted with eight rockets, the rails of which have the correct T section, a point often overlooked even on more expensive kits, two bombs or long range drop tanks; the Mk VI can use either the bombs or tanks whilst the Mk II has no under-wing stores. The lower wing panels have pre-marked holes to accommodate these alternatives so it must be remembered to drill out the holes before fitting the lower panels to the wing tops. While in this area it is also worth reminding the reader to fit the landing lights in the under surfaces and paint their reflectors silver inside the top surfaces before fixing the two parts together.

Surface detail is extremely fine and includes bomb bays, ammunition bays, entry doors, access doors to equipment, fuel filler caps, downward identification lights, navigation lights and, of course, control surfaces. Because of its outstanding quality this kit will feature prominently in the conversions since a lot of detail work that is required in the Matchbox kit is already included in the Airfix one. This is not meant to be a slight on Matchbox whose kit is very good and, of course, aimed at a lower price bracket, but if you can afford to buy supplies of both then you have the best of both worlds when it comes to cannibalising and thus keeping extra work to a minimum.

Matchbox kit No PK-116

Manufacturers, often quite unknown to each other, embark on the design and production of identical models and when they are released enthusiasts groan and ask why they could not have got together and produced different versions of the particular subject.

This is, of course, not always possible especially as commercial plans are often very closely guarded secrets; whether or not Matchbox and Airfix knew of each other's intentions is not the concern of this narrative, but in the case of the Mosquito they both came up with entirely different versions and the modeller has benefitted.

The Matchbox 1:72 scale kit provides alternative parts for an NF 30 of 85 Squadron RAF and a Mk IX bomber of 105 Squadron based at Marham, not Marnham as stated on the box artwork. Both these aircraft used stage-two Merlins with chin intakes so immediately the major problem of converting the single-stage engines as provided on the Airfix kit is disposed of. Unfortunately both companies' tool makers have tackled the engine nacelles in different ways so it is not just a case of swopping engines; but more of that later.

The Mosquito NF 30 has what is known as the Universal radar nose and the flat-screened canopy, whilst the B IX has a glazed nose and pointed-screened canopy. Matchbox chose to mould the main fuselage sections to the front of the cockpit and the alternative nose sections forward from that point. This means that there is a rather prominent join line on either model but this is easily filled with a proprietary filler and sanded smooth. The alternative nose sections, parts 27/28 for the NF 30 and 29 to 32 for the B IX, come in separate halves, so anyone who has a Mattel vac-form can use these parts to form his own conversion pieces. Marrying the Matchbox noses to the Airfix kit is not difficult but it is not advisable to use the demarcation line on the Airfix kit, but rather to cut the fuselage just forward of the wing root and use the whole Matchbox nose section. This work will be covered where necessary in the relevant conversion subjects.

As far as accuracy is concerned it is easy to be over critical, especially when commenting on the fuselage length which is marginally too long and not worth correcting, but criticism of the over-all surface detail is perhaps valid. The Mosquito had a very smooth surface finish and this must be kept in mind when modelling it, but it is hard to understand why Matchbox included the equipment hatch aft of the starboard wing and just below the fuselage strengthening strake, but omitted any form of entry hatch, the dinghy stowage panel aft of the cockpit on the fuselage top and other prominent inspection panels which are clearly detailed on their competitor's offerings. While still on the fuselage, it is certainly worth pointing out that the strake on the starboard side is far too prominent and too long. It should be reduced by 4 mm at the front end then rubbed down with wet-and-dry until a more scale-like appearance is achieved; this work must be done on any Mosquito which uses the Matchbox kit as its basis. Other fuselage panelling can be added with a steel rule and scriber after studying photographs and drawings, but be careful as some aircraft had minor variations and the previously mentioned dinghy stowage behind the cockpit was not always prominent. The bomb-bays must

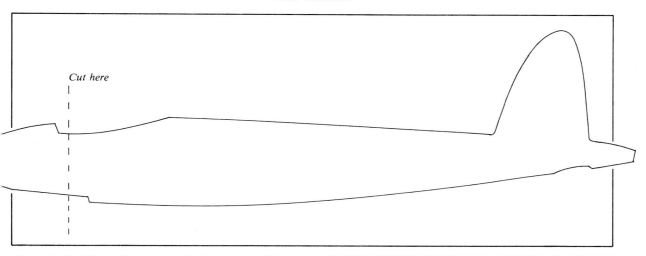

Cut here

Above *Airfix 1:72 scale fuselage showing the point at which the nose is removed in order to fit the Matchbox nose.*

Right top *NF 30 engine chin intake built up on the Airfix engine or a modified Matchbox engine,* **centre** *small-style 'thimble' nose on the Mk XII and XIII,* **below** *'Universal' nose as in the Matchbox kit.*

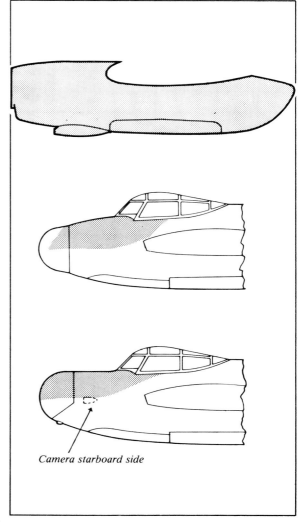

Camera starboard side

be included and the blister covering the elevator actuator on the port side just below the fin/rudder should be increased in size. The engines are rivet free which is a good thing, but again they lack some detail and are greatly enhanced by careful work with a scriber or the pointed end of a modelling knife. The intakes at the front can be improved by being hollowed out and painted black inside, this work must be executed with extreme care as it is very easy to cut away too much plastic and damage the side walls.

The wings have the control surfaces, navigation lights and filling points deeply engraved, but no attempt has been made to reproduce the honeycomb of the radiators, or provide landing lights, although the latter are shown on the box artwork for both versions.

As in the Airfix kit, exhaust shrouds or open stacks are available, the latter illustrating the point made earlier as they are correct for six-stack systems as used on these aircraft. The propellers are a big disappointment as they cannot seem to make up their mind as to whether or not they should be ordinary or paddle blades. The NF 30 used the latter type but the B IX can be seen with either, those in the Matchbox kit are more akin to paddle blades, but if you can afford it the answer is to use spares from the Airfix kit. As far as the undercarriage goes, this is by no means as detailed as it might be and the wheel door guides have been completely omitted from the oleos, the wheels themselves are correct in diameter but have very little central hub, which is a feature easily seen on the real aircraft. The internal cockpit detail is very poor and the floor location is far too low if the kit instructions are followed.

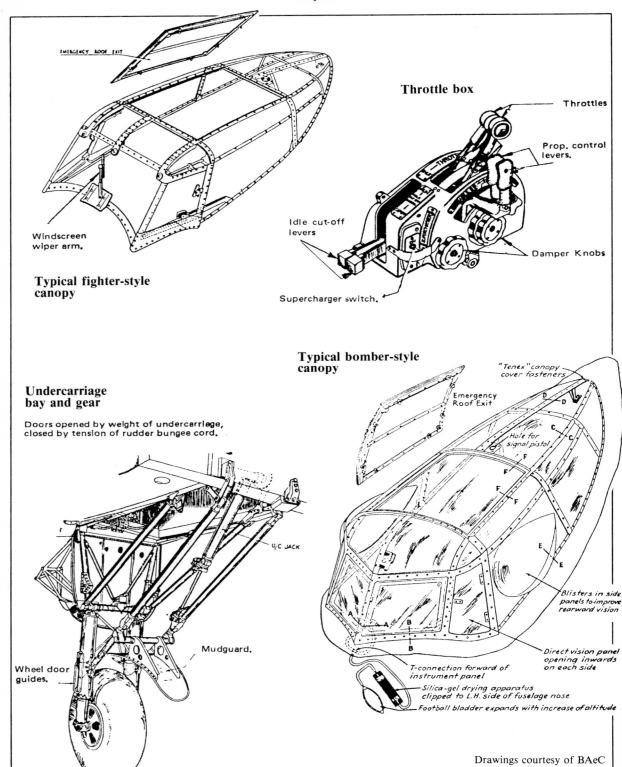

EMERGENCY ROOF EXIT

Windscreen
wiper arm.

**Typical fighter-style
canopy**

Throttle box

Throttles

Prop. control
levers.

Idle cut-off
levers

Damper Knobs

Supercharger switch.

**Typical bomber-style
canopy**

**Undercarriage
bay and gear**

Doors opened by weight of undercarriage,
closed by tension of rudder bungee cord.

U/C JACK.

Mudguard.

Wheel door
guides.

"Tenex" canopy
cover fasteners

Emergency
Roof Exit

Hole for
signal pistol

Blisters in side
panels to improve
rearward vision

Direct vision panel
opening inwards
on each side

T-connection forward of
instrument panel

Silica-gel drying apparatus
clipped to L.H. side of fuselage nose

Football bladder expands with increase of altitude

Drawings courtesy of BAeC

Wherever I used the Matchbox fuselage I chose to make a completely new cockpit floor 1 mm wider than part 6, and located it just below the wing root locating slot, this effectively raised both seats to a more accurate level and was far more acceptable in the completed models. There is no instrument panel, but a bulkhead on which one can be fitted is located in the alternative nose sections. The general comments made about improving the interior of the Airfix kit also, of course, apply to this one and, again, are very much a matter of personal choice. The bomber-type control yoke should be replaced by those making the NF 30 and who want to be as accurate as they can. The cockpit canopies provided in this kit are useful when it comes to conversion work, the only drawbacks being that the lower line of both need some alteration to enable either to fit the Airfix kit, and the blister on the top of the bomber canopy (part 25) is an embarrassment as it was not by any means fitted to all aircraft and is hard to remove. It is a great pity that it was not supplied as a separate item as are the side blisters, then it could have been added or omitted as required. The only other point which should be mentioned on the debit side is the complete absence of the two blisters under the wings at the mid-chord point where they join the fuselage. Modellers who tend to neglect the under surfaces of their models will probably not worry too much about these, but they should be added either from shaped plastic sprue applied with liquid cement, or made-up from body filler. In my case I used Milliput which I find to be the best filler currently available as it is easy to work with, dries very hard and does not flake or feather when worked on.

Wing long-range tanks or bombs are provided for the two versions so, like the Airfix kit, this one does provide plenty of very useful material for the spares box. This kit is a very useful one for the Mosquito modeller; with some diligent work it can be made into a very acceptable replica and certainly provides many useful components for those who wish to use it to cross-kit. When assessing it, remember that it is in a lower price range than the Airfix kit and cannot therefore be expected to come up to the same standard of detail.

Frog/Novo kit No F 187

This completes the quartet of 1:72 scale Mosquito kits issued, but unlike the other three, it is now not too easy to come by. It has been included because at the time of writing it was still available under the original Frog label, and by the time this appears in print, is likely to have reappeared in the Novo range. Should the latter arrangement not materialise then the kit will obviously become a collector's item and more a subject for those whose hobby is to collect kits rather than build them. However, it is worth some mention since for a long time it was the only kit to compete with the original and new Airfix offerings, and certainly has points of considerable merit. The kit includes alternative parts for a Mk IV bomber with markings for the aircraft flown by Wing Commander John Wooldridge, one-time CO of 105 Squadron RAF, and a Mk VI fighter-bomber of 1 Squadron RAAF in SEAC markings. This choice means that the pointed- and flat-screened canopies are provided and, in this case, the former is very useful as it does not have a top blister moulded to it and therefore provides many more possibilities for bomber conversions than the Matchbox canopy. Alternative noses are, of course, necessary and in the Frog kit the designer has elected to provide a complete fuselage with the clear bomber nose, and the solid fighter nose as a separate moulding. Unlike the Airfix kit, the separation line is just forward of the wing roots which does in fact make it easier to use the alternative NF Universal nose from the Matchbox kit if you want to. This separation line is in exactly the position required on the Airfix fuselage for marrying the Matchbox noses to that kit, but more of that later.

The entry hatch under the nose for the B IV is shown as a raised panel, so work in sanding this down and re-scribing it is a must, the same comment also applies to the equipment hatch on the starboard side of the fuselage aft of the wing trailing edge. Oddly enough, the dinghy stowage hatch aft of the cockpit canopy is scribed and the only work needed in this area is the reduction in size of the fuselage strengthening band which passes around the diameter of the fuselage. Whilst this is being reduced the lateral strengthener on the fuselage starboard side can also be sanded off as it is the wrong length and far too high on the fuselage.

Microstrip can be used to replace the circular strengthener if it is removed completely and a piece of stretched sprue 35 mm long, of which 8 mm from the wing trailing edge, goes under the wing surface, can be used to replace the lateral strengthener. The B IV bomb-bay doors have the two circular windows which were featured on this aircraft but a similar window is not provided for the entry hatch, and should be added. The position of the trailing aerial fairlead is too high on the fuselage side and should be filled and replaced by a drilled hole 3 mm to starboard of the centre-line. Unfortunately the most serious problem with this kit is that the wings are placed far too high on the fuselage. The root positions practically break the lower line of the cockpit which makes any model completed from this kit look a little odd. The work involved in correcting this is not worthwhile especially as there are now better kits available. One other serious error is in the shape of the leading edge of the fin, this results in an entirely uncharacteristic DH appendage. Correction is possible by replacing with a fin/rudder from the early Airfix kit, or a new one built from plastic card. Before leaving the fuselage it is worth mentioning the small bulge moulded to the starboard fuselage side (part 2), this is under the wing centre-section and does not appear on all aircraft, but it is present on the T III in the RAF Museum and can be seen on photographs of other aircraft.

The cockpit interior consists of the usual rather shapeless seats but in this case, the bulkhead carrying the instrument panel is the correct shape although only six instruments are engraved in the area where this is contained. The provision of alternate control columns has not been overlooked, neither has the detail of the anti-shimmy tailwheel, although the latter has a raised ridge around its periphery instead of a groove.

The wings and engines are the correct shape although the purist will argue that the nacelles are a shade too shallow, but the open exhaust stacks are incorrect and should not be used. Still on the power units, the propeller blades are moulded integrally with the spinners and are a cross between standard and paddle blades. The undercarriage legs and mudguards are a little heavy but the oleos do include the wheel door guides which were omitted by Matchbox. A complement of eight underwing rockets are included but these have overscale fins and their carrier rails are incorrect.

The transparencies, which have already been briefly mentioned, are very good and although at first glance the bomber nose glazing looks to be too short and pinched, it is in fact reasonably accurate. Comparison of photographs indicates that there could well have been considerable discrepancy in the manufacture of this component on the real aircraft, and as it was blown Perspex this is probably quite true. By careful filing of the lower edges, the Frog canopies can be adapted to fit the other 1:72 scale models and they are well worth looking for if the chance of rummaging through another modeller's spares box arises. Over-all, this is not a good kit by present day standards, but it does yield many usable parts for the modeller who wants to spend a lot of time making models of Mosquitoes without having to resort to a lot of scratch-building. If you see one, buy it; one way or another it will be a good investment.

Monogram kit No PA 129-200, 6849 and 5408

For a long time this was the only 1:48 scale kit of the Mosquito available and was issued under the three part numbers shown with variations in box art, and improvements in some detail parts in the later kit (No 5408). It has been around for nearly as long as the original Airfix 1:72 kit but the quality of Monogram tool making and moulding is far superior to that shown in this model's contemporaries. Progress has, of course, brought a great raising of standards but this early kit will stand competition with the latest offerings, whereas we have already seen that its original competitors will not.

Unfortunately there are some serious errors in the kit and putting them right is not easy, as in many cases correcting one mistake creates a problem in another direction. The kit contains enough parts to produce quarter scale models of four different aircraft, these and the associate decals for them are: a Mk IV bomber of 105 Squadron RAF, serial DZ378, GB:K; Mk II night intruder of 23 Squadron RAF, serial DZ230, YP:A; a Mk VI fighter bomber of 487 RNZAF Squadron, serial MM417, EG:T (this aircraft has the same markings as

those included in the original Airfix 1:72 scale model); and finally a Mk II night fighter, serial DD609, of an unidentified home defence unit.

The main fuselage mouldings have the bomber nose moulded as an integral part but the separation point for the alternative 'solid' nose is clearly marked. This is on a line just forward of the cockpit and wing leading edge and means that part B9, the cockpit floor, also has to have its front end cut off if the fighter or fighter-bomber versions are chosen. Another interesting feature of this kit is that the bomb-bay and undercarriage doors, are moulded in the closed position, but have been marked very deeply along their hinge lines to facilitate removal. Having provided this, Monogram have not overlooked the bomb-bay interior, this being fully detailed on the base of part B9. The small circular windows which were a feature of the Mk IV have been omitted from the front ends of the bomb doors and the crew entry hatch, but they can be added by the same technique as that described later in the chapter on detailing the large Revell kit. The cockpit interior consists of the usual seats, which can be greatly improved by removing the moulded harnesses, replacing them with drafting tape or thin plastic card, building up the sides of the seats and re-shaping the headrests. The instrument panel is scribed on to part B13 and is a good representation of a Mosquito panel. Careful painting and highlighting of the instruments by the dry brushing technique pays dividends on this component. The cockpit walls are bare and should have the appropriate black boxes, associate accessories, wiring and controls added, since they are clearly visible through the very clear canopy. If the crew entry hatch is going to be cut out and shown in the open position, remember to cut away part of the cockpit floor otherwise the hatch will just show entry to a solid-roofed compartment! Alternative fighter or bomber control columns are included, but there are no separate exhausts so only the shrouded versions can be modelled unless you want to scratch-build open exhausts, similarly only the standard propeller blades are included so if this kit is to form the basis of conversions using the paddle blades, these will have to be built on to the existing propeller boss.

Because the four versions chosen are all quite different, alternative weapons and armament are a must and Monogram have duly obliged with rockets, wing tanks, wing bombs, internal bombs, nose armament and radar aerials. All components are crisply moulded and fit well, but it is in attention to general accuracy where problems occur.

Earlier I mentioned that it is not always necessary or desirable to cary out very small changes as in many cases these are not noticeable; in the case of the Monogram 1:48 scale kit the modeller is faced with a combination of problems. A model made straight from the kit does look like a Mosquito but even those with only a rudimentary knowledge of the original are likely to comment that 'something looks wrong'. A contributory reason

The .303 Browning installation on the Mk II

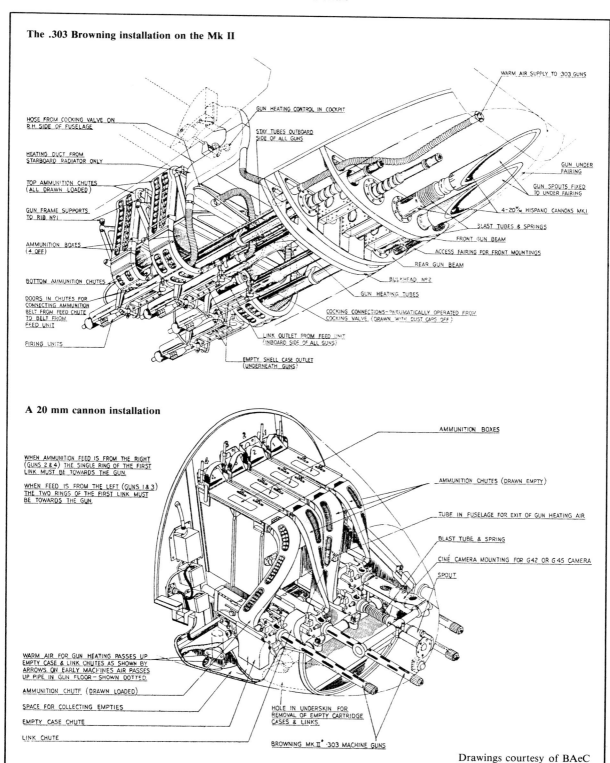

WARM AIR SUPPLY TO .303 GUNS

GUN HEATING CONTROL IN COCKPIT

STAY TUBES OUTBOARD SIDE OF ALL GUNS

GUN UNDER FAIRING

GUN SPOUTS FIXED TO UNDER FAIRING

4-20% HISPANO CANNONS MK.I

BLAST TUBES & SPRINGS

FRONT GUN BEAM

ACCESS FAIRING FOR FRONT MOUNTINGS

REAR GUN BEAM

BULKHEAD No.2

GUN HEATING TUBES

COCKING CONNECTIONS-PNEUMATICALLY OPERATED FROM COCKING VALVE. (DRAWN WITH DUST CAPS OFF)

LINK OUTLET FROM FEED UNIT (INBOARD SIDE OF ALL GUNS)

EMPTY SHELL CASE OUTLET (UNDERNEATH GUNS)

HOSE FROM COCKING VALVE ON R.H. SIDE OF FUSELAGE

HEATING DUCT FROM STARBOARD RADIATOR ONLY

TOP AMMUNITION CHUTES (ALL DRAWN LOADED)

GUN FRAME SUPPORTS TO RIB No.1

AMMUNITION BOXES (4 OFF)

BOTTOM AMMUNITION CHUTES

DOORS IN CHUTES FOR CONNECTING AMMUNITION BELT FROM FEED CHUTE TO BELT FROM FEED UNIT

FIRING UNITS

A 20 mm cannon installation

AMMUNITION BOXES

WHEN AMMUNITION FEED IS FROM THE RIGHT (GUNS 2 & 4) THE SINGLE RING OF THE FIRST LINK MUST BE TOWARDS THE GUN.

WHEN FEED IS FROM THE LEFT (GUNS 1 & 3) THE TWO RINGS OF THE FIRST LINK MUST BE TOWARDS THE GUN.

AMMUNITION CHUTES (DRAWN EMPTY)

TUBE IN FUSELAGE FOR EXIT OF GUN HEATING AIR

BLAST TUBE & SPRING

CINÉ CAMERA MOUNTING FOR G42 OR G45 CAMERA

SPOUT

WARM AIR FOR GUN HEATING PASSES UP EMPTY CASE & LINK CHUTES AS SHOWN BY ARROWS. ON EARLY MACHINES AIR PASSES UP PIPE IN GUN FLOOR - SHOWN DOTTED.

AMMUNITION CHUTE (DRAWN LOADED)

SPACE FOR COLLECTING EMPTIES

EMPTY CASE CHUTE

LINK CHUTE

HOLE IN UNDERSKIN FOR REMOVAL OF EMPTY CARTRIDGE CASES & LINKS.

BROWNING MK.II* .303 MACHINE GUNS

Drawings courtesy of BAeC

for this is that the fin/rudder is nearly one scale foot too tall and this tends to give the rear end of the model the appearance of a caricature of the aircraft. This error is one which *must* be rectified and the only way to do it is completely to remove the fin/rudder from the fuselage and cut off 5 mm from the base before cementing it back into position. This surgery results in the trim tab hinge being moved too near the fuselage top-line so this must also be replaced in a central position. The base-line of the rudder will be removed during the shortening exercise so must be re-scribed once the fin/rudder has set. If only this error is corrected the over-all appearance is improved but the model will still have a 'lean and hungry look' resulting from the fact that in plan view the fuselage is too narrow. To correct this leads to many major problems. Only the very skilled and experienced modeller should set out to undertake the corrective work needed, and such a man might well feel that starting from scratch by moulding a new fuselage is the better answer. For those who want to accept the challenge, this is what is required. The fuselage is far too slab-sided in the area of the wing roots so a more circular cross-section must be built up using Milliput or some other filler, this must continue to the tail section as this area is also somewhat flat where it should be rounded. If the clear-nosed bomber version is being modelled, the nose windows are marginally oversize, the easiest way to correct these being to insert the clear parts, then sand the whole smooth and, at the painting stage, reduce the area of the glazing. The fairlead for the trailing aerial is positioned incorrectly on the centre-line and the hole provided should be filled and a new one drilled offset to starboard.

The narrow fuselage in the kit results in the engines being too close together which leads to the propeller blades being fractionally short; widening the fuselage goes some way to correcting the error since the wings do not now fit into the slots provided but butt against the re-modelled fuselage contours. This does result in an error occurring in the span, which is correct if the kit is built from the box, but too great if the fuselage is modified in diameter. The solution is to remove 5 mm from each wing-tip and re-shape it with wet-and-dry. Whilst doing this it is also a good idea to fill the outer line of the ailerons and re-scribe this 3 mm inboard. Additional work is needed at the roots, this being the extension of the radiators and the repositioning of the fairing under the centre sections. The work involved is considerable and once undertaken there are no short cuts, so it is very advisable to think hard before starting such a major task. The only other area where there is a major discrepancy is in the engine nacelles aft of the line scribed at the forward end of the undercarriage bay. From this point to the trailing edge, the nacelles are too tapered and should be built up once again with your favourite filler. This is a difficult task as it results in the loss of some surface detail which is hard to replace by scribing. I chose to use the Monogram kit for the conversion to the prototype which follows later, as this involves removing the rear part of the nacelles and leads to a partial solution to this particular problem. The final point worth mentioning is that the wheels provided are marginally too narrow and can be corrected by inserting a plastic card disc between the two halves before cementing them together. Apart from one or two incorrectly inscribed panel lines, especially around the engine nacelles, the kit is very finely detailed and certainly worth building. Although the shortcomings listed seem to be considerable, a correct perspective must be retained, and if only the minor work listed such as the shortening of the fin/rudder, re-scribing the aileron outer hinge line, re-marking some of the panels, and adding interior detail are carried out, the result will be a worthwhile quarter scale Mosquito.

An FB VI of the Israeli Air Force. It has silver dope over-all, a blue rudder and spinners, and the exhaust area is stylised black. The code is in black and the national markings are blue on a white disc. (See page 81).

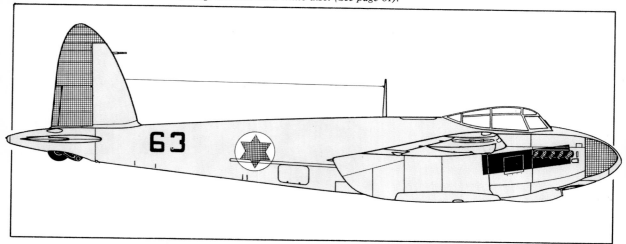

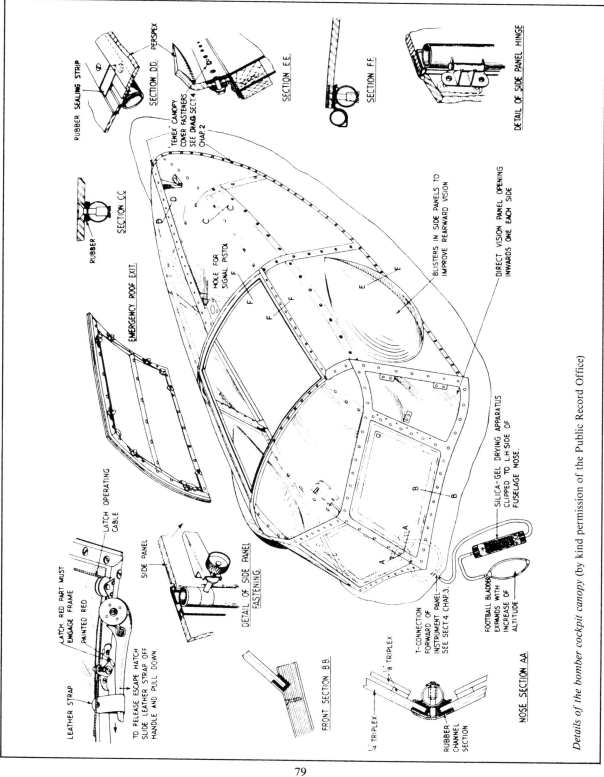

RUBBER SEALING STRIP

SECTION DD. PERSPEX

SECTION EE.

SECTION FF.

DETAIL OF SIDE PANEL HINGE

SECTION CC

RUBBER

EMERGENCY ROOF EXIT.

TENEX CANOPY
COVER FASTENERS
SEE DIAG SECT.4
CHAP 2

BLISTERS IN SIDE PANELS TO
IMPROVE REARWARD VISION

DIRECT VISION PANEL OPENING
INWARDS ONE EACH SIDE

HOLE FOR
SIGNAL PISTOL

SILICA-GEL DRYING APPARATUS
CLIPPED TO L.H. SIDE OF
FUSELAGE NOSE.

FOOTBALL BLADDER
EXPANDS WITH
INCREASE OF
ALTITUDE

LATCH OPERATING
CABLE

LATCH RED PART MUST
ENGAGE FRAME
PAINTED RED

SIDE PANEL

LEATHER STRAP

TO RELEASE ESCAPE HATCH
SLIDE LEATHER STRAP OFF
HANDLE AND PULL DOWN

DETAIL OF SIDE PANEL
FASTENING

FRONT SECTION BB.

T-CONNECTION
FORWARD OF
INSTRUMENT PANEL
SEE SECT.4 CHAP.3.

¼ TRIPLEX

⅛ TRIPLEX

RUBBER
CHANNEL
SECTION

NOSE SECTION AA

Details of the bomber cockpit canopy (by kind permission of the Public Record Office)

79

The cockpit equipment layout in the Mosquito IX (by kind permission of the Public Record Office)

Key to cockpit layout

I.	Instruments flood lamp	20.	First aid equipment	42.	Trailing aerial winch
2.	Steering Indicator	21.	Hydraulic hand pump	43.	Chart table
3.	Intercooler indicator push switches	22.	Incendiary bombs stowage	44.	Camera control box, wedge plates and lead stowage
4.	Compass	23.	Master and ignition switches		
5.	Compass floodlamp and dimmer switch	24.	Pilot's oxygen regulator	45.	Observer's wireless and intercom. switch
6.	Pilot's cold air punkah louvre	25.	Bomb container Jettison switch		
7.	External fuel tanks jettison switch	26.	Bomb jettison handle	46.	Observer's oxygen regulator
8.	Tail trim indicator	27.	Aileron trim control and Indicator	47.	Pencil holder
9.	Pilot's intercommunication plug	28.	Windscreen de-icer pump	48.	Observer's cold air control
10.	U/c and engine data plates and compass deviation card holder	29.	Fireman's axe	49.	Radiator flap control and indicators
		30.	Syko apparatus stowage	50.	Oxygen high pressure valve
11.	Bomb sight control panel (B.Mk. IX only)	31.	Observer's oxygen pipe	51.	Junction box ''B''
		32.	Knee cushion	52.	Identification lamp signalling switch box
12.	Engine control box	33.	Ladder stowage		
13.	Fire extinguisher (hand operated)	34.	Signal cartridge stowage	53.	Outside air temperature indicator
14.	Pilot's wireless and Intercom. switch	35.	Emergency selector valve	54.	Dimmer switches for instrument and chart table floodlamps
15.	Pilot's oxygen pipe	36.	Drift sight		
16.	Radio controller	37.	Drift sight control and computor stowage	55.	Propeller feathering switches
17.	Cabin heater control			56.	Beam approach visual indicator
18.	Sanitary funnel and container	38.	Hydraulic hand pump handle	57.	Time of flight clock
19.	Torch	40.	Camera heater control	58.	Observer's cold air punkah louvre
19A.	Pilot's distress and beam approach SW.	41.	Observer's intercommunication plug	59.	Vacuum control cock

Airfix kit 06100-7

When this book was first mooted Airfix had announced that they would be adding a 1:48 scale kit of the Mosquito to their range. At the time of writing this had not reached full-scale production although it is likely to be generally available before the book is published. Airfix were kind enough to supply a very early test shot but I felt that it was grossly unfair to them to pass comment about this or to include it in any depth since it would be easy to be critical about something which might not necessarily be present on the final production kit. Having made that quite clear I feel it is also only fair to state that the test shot looks very good indeed with plenty of detail especially in the cockpit area, good fit of parts, and very accurate over-all dimensions.

The kit is basically an FB VI and obviously owes a lot to the 1:72 scale offering from the same company, having the same fidelity of detail plus refinement in areas which were criciticised by reviewers of the smaller model. Alternative markings for a fighter or Coastal Command aircraft are included as are optional armament and underwing stores.

The test shot I received certainly captured the feel of the original and will undoubtedly form the basis of many conversions for the 1:48 scale addict. Most of the details given in later chapters relating to conversions will also apply to this kit, but do not get any comments concerning outline accuracy confused, for this 1:48 scale model does not have too narrow a fuselage, nor too short a fin, it is, in fact, very precise and a credit to the mould designers and makers.

Revell kit No H-180

This is the only 1:32 scale Mosquito kit available and although it has been in production for a number of years, it is still one of the most accurate, suffering only minor errors which are easily corrected. The kit provides no alternative parts for different versions so only the B IV can be produced without conversion work, and the markings provided for this are for DZ353, GB:E of 105 Squadron RAF. This kit features in the next chapter during which many of what some consider to be its shortcomings will be mentioned, so there is little point in duplicating comment here.

Before going on to look at the Revell kit in some detail it is worth commenting on its conversion potential. Conversion to a solid-nosed fighter, intruder or night fighter, should not give the average modeller any major headaches. There are many ways the solid nose can be tackled and probably the most satisfactory is to plug the side nose windows with plastic card, attach the clear nose transparency, then cover the whole area with filler which is sanded to shape when it is dry. The V-shaped opening on the top decking, which accommodates the pointed windscreen, is filled with plastic card and the joins are then hidden with filler. Internal cockpit detail is changed to that associated with the fighter versions, the most obvious of which would be the inclusion of a radar screen on night fighters and the single-grip control column in lieu of the wheeled version used in the bomber. The biggest problem is the moulding of a new canopy but the method every modeller worth his salt is familar with — that of carving of a wooden master then pressing heated acetate into a female mould with it — will produce the desired result. Versions using the open exhaust stacks present no problems as these are included in the Revell kit, but those where six stacks instead of five are needed will mean some scratch-building. This is not difficult as the additional exhaust can be based on those included in the kit or, indeed, the kit parts can be used to form the master from which extra pipes can be moulded. The technique of using casting rubber to form a master from existing kit parts, then using this master to mould in resin or other material, is a growing part of the conversion and scratch-building hobby and one well worth perfecting. Failing this, the exhaust stacks can be made from sprue or even soft solder, which is very easy to work with and looks very convincing. Propeller blades will also need to be scratch-built where the paddle type are required but this is by no means difficult work in this scale. The blades included in the Airfix kit are ideal as guides and give an impression of the shape, so it is simply a matter of studying these and basing the new ones on them. Once again the quickest way would be to carve one blade from hard wood, then make a rubber mould and cast the others in resin from this.

On some Mosquitoes it will be necessary to lengthen the carburettor intake and this is done by adding sprue to the exisiting parts then carving it to shape before fixing the intake guard to the front. Aircraft fitted with two-stage Merlins present different problems as the nacelles have to be lengthened and re-shaped. This is done by cutting off the forward part of the nacelles at the firewall bulkhead, then adding six scale inches with laminated plastic card or balsa, attaching the front end to this, then fairing the assembly with filler before sanding smooth. The chin intake for the intercooler is built up on the nacelle with filler and the position of the carburettor intake modified in line with drawings and photographs of the particular aircraft chosen as the modelling subject.

There are many variations to the basic theme available to the modeller, and much of the pleasure in producing any conversion is the research involved in collecting material and deciding the best way to carry out the work needed. The outline shape of the Mosquito did not vary a great deal: different noses, bulged bomb-bays, camera ports, additional strengthening ribs, cockpit variations and minor modifications, all contribute to make various Marks slightly different, and not every one will appeal to all modellers; those chosen by me to feature in the relevant part of this book, are purely a personal choice but will, I hope, give some guidance as to methods which can be adapted to any variant chosen by the reader. Similarly the methods and changes made apply to any scale, although the majority included are to the universally accepted 1:72 scale.

Chapter Eight

Adding detail

It is generally accepted that the amount of detail which can be added to any scale model is inversely proportional to the scale chosen. The amount of fine detail which can be added to the Revell 1:32 scale kit would, if included on say a 1:72 scale model, tend to make the smaller aircraft look cluttered and uninteresting. However, it is good practice to build at least one large-scale, super-detailed model and from that decide on just how much it is prudent to add to smaller scales. The question of storage space for completed models is an age old one, and it is a fairly safe assumption that there are not too many modellers who have room to keep many 1:32 scale aircraft, especially in an average domestic environment. In view of this common problem all the conversions which follow in the next chapter, apart from the prototype Mosquito, are based on 1:72 scale kits, but since the Revell kit is readily available and attractive it forms the ideal basis for super-detailing. Reference material is an essential part of the serious modeller's library, there is plenty available on the Mosquito and this is listed elsewhere; but it seems worth mentioning the Arms and Armour Press reproduction of the *Mosquito II Manual*. This publication is the official Air Publication for the Mosquito F Mk II, NF Mk XII and NF Mk XVII; it contains a wealth of useful information most of which is, of course, applicable to those aircraft mentioned, but it also has many parts which apply to Mosquitoes generally. Any modeller who intends to devote a lot of time and effort to modelling many varieties of Mosquito will find this publication indispensible, while even the casual enthusiast who wants to add just that little bit extra to his efforts will certainly find it useful to read. Much of the detail I have included on the Revell model

has been gleaned from this book's pages as well as from drawings supplied by British Aerospace.

One criticism levelled at the Revell kit is that it seems to be acres of plain plastic with very little surface detail, but this is totally unfair as the Mosquito was a very smooth-skinned wooden aircraft and *had* very little surface detail! The fuselage cross-section does tend to be rather egg-shaped instead of elliptical but this is easily rectified by judicious use of wet-and-dry on the top of the fuselage.

The size of this model gives the fastidious modeller plenty of scope not only to add extra detail but also to include individual touches which will make his model just that bit different from the next man's. In tackling the 1:32 scale kit, I decided to combine the addition of detail with touches which appealed to me but will not necessarily be the choice of every reader, so once again we are back to the question of personal choice.

Having decided to open as many hatches as I could, I started by cutting out the bomb-bay doors, crew entry hatch, and the electrical/oxygen services hatch on the starboard fuselage side. This work is best carried out with a modelling knife fitted with a new No 11 blade; from experience I would suggest that you work slowly and follow the etched lines on the moulding and *do not* attempt to cut through the plastic in one go. If the bomb-bay doors are removed first the piece of plastic remaining between the forward end and the crew entry hatch is very narrow, it is essential therefore that the fuselage half is held very firmly otherwise it tends to twist and the blade can be diverted from the true cutting line. Once the doors and hatches are removed, place them on one side and tidy-up the fuselage openings with

The Revell 1:32 scale Mosquito Mk IV. Note the displaced control surfaces, exposed exhaust stacks and open hatches. The rear ends of the engine nacelles have been reshaped as detailed in the text (Ian Jebbett ARPS).

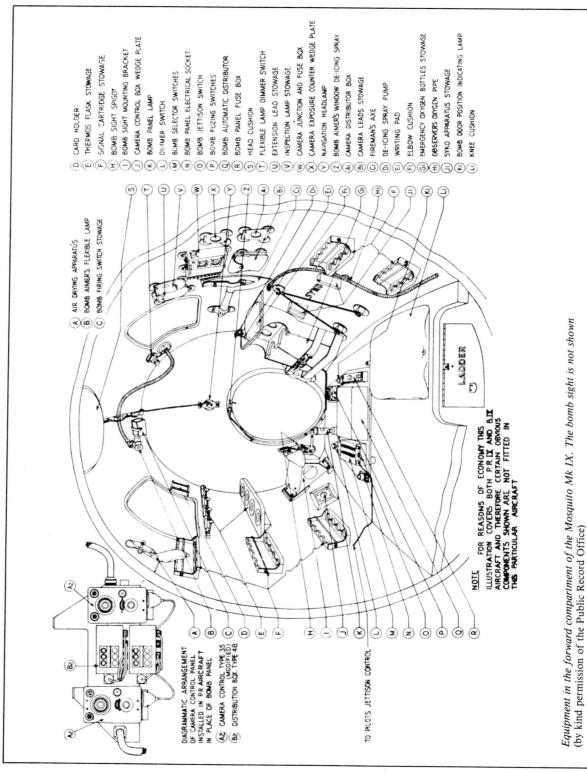

(D) CARD HOLDER
(E) THERMOS FLASK STOWAGE
(F) SIGNAL CARTRIDGE STOWAGE
(H) BOMB SIGHT SPIGOT
(I) BOMB SIGHT MOUNTING BRACKET
(J) CAMERA CONTROL BOX WEDGE PLATE
(K) BOMB PANEL LAMP
(L) DIMMER SWITCH
(M) BOMB SELECTOR SWITCHES
(N) BOMB PANEL ELECTRICAL SOCKET
(O) BOMB JETTISON SWITCH
(P) BOMB FUZING SWITCHES
(Q) BOMB AUTOMATIC DISTRIBUTOR
(R) BOMB PANEL FUSE BOX
(S) HEAD CUSHION
(T) FLEXIBLE LAMP DIMMER SWITCH
(U) EXTENSION LEAD STOWAGE
(V) INSPECTION LAMP STOWAGE
(W) CAMERA JUNCTION AND FUSE BOX
(X) CAMERA EXPOSURE COUNTER WEDGE PLATE
(Y) NAVIGATION HEADLAMP
(Z) BOMB AIMER'S WINDOW DE-ICING SPRAY
(A1) CAMERA DISTRIBUTOR BOX
(B1) CAMERA LEADS STOWAGE
(G1) FIREMAN'S AXE
(D1) DE-ICING SPRAY PUMP
(E1) WRITING PAD
(F1) ELBOW CUSHION
(G1) EMERGENCY OXYGEN BOTTLES STOWAGE
(H1) OBSERVER'S OXYGEN PIPE
(J1) SYKO APPARATUS STOWAGE
(K1) BOMB DOOR POSITION INDICATING LAMP
(L1) KNEE CUSHION

(A) AIR DRYING APPARATUS
(B) BOMB AIMER'S FLEXIBLE LAMP
(C) BOMB FIRING SWITCH STOWAGE

DIAGRAMMATIC ARRANGEMENT
OF CAMERA CONTROL PANEL
INSTALLED IN PR AIRCRAFT
IN PLACE OF BOMB PANEL

(A2) CAMERA CONTROL TYPE 35 (MODIFIED)
(B2) DISTRIBUTION BOX TYPE 46

TO PILOTS JETTISON CONTROL

NOTE FOR REASONS OF ECONOMY THIS
ILLUSTRATION COVERS BOTH P.R IX AND B.IX
AIRCRAFT AND THEREFORE CERTAIN OBVIOUS
COMPONENTS SHOWN ARE NOT FITTED IN
THIS PARTICULAR AIRCRAFT

Equipment in the forward compartment of the Mosquito Mk IX. The bomb sight is not shown
(by kind permission of the Public Record Office)

wet-and-dry, but be careful not to remove too much plastic otherwise it becomes obvious that the parts removed will not fit where they are intended to. The crew entry hatch and bomb-bay doors now have holes drilled in them to accommodate the windows (which are shown as decals in the kits). The decal sheet serves a useful purpose in this respect since the solid black discs give the exact sizes of the holes required. I started by marking the correct positions for these windows, then drilled a small hole in the centre and gradually enlarged this with bigger drills, finishing with a rat-tailed file. A search through the spares box produced a correct diameter window for the crew entry hatch, but nothing for the bomb-bay doors, so the latter were cut from clear plastic which started life as a stand in an Airfix kit; any other suitable clear material will, of course, do just as well. These windows were not fitted into place until further work had been carried out. Dealing with the entry hatch first, this comprised a 2 mm wide strip of .010 plastic card cemented around the edges of the inside of the door, and the fitting of hinges and handles. The latter were made from stretched sprue with white PVA glue grips which were painted yellow with black stripes when they were dry. The photograph on page 111 shows this hatch as fitted to the Mk 35 at Salisbury Hall, it is very unlikely that the bar across the window was fitted to all versions using this method of crew entry.

Plastic card strengthening ribs were then made and fitted to the front and rear ends of the bomb doors and, when they were firmly set, lightening holes were drilled into them; the retraction jacks for the doors were made from sprue and added when the doors were finally cemented to the aircraft. Having opened the hatches it is essential that interior detail is added, otherwise all that has been achieved is a clear view of blank plastic! Front and rear bomb-bay bulkheads were made from .020 in plastic card and cemented in position in the port fuselage half (part 17). A roof was made from the same material and detailed with sprue and Microstrip before being fitted to the top of the two bulkheads. Attention was then turned to the compartment on the starboard side, entry to which is gained by the hatch already removed. This compartment is made from .020 in plastic card using the formers shown (see photograph) and cemented firmly in position; do not worry too much if the bulkheads have not been cut accurately enough to follow the internal fuselage curves, as any gaps can be filled with Milliput and sanded smooth. Oxygen bottles can be made from suitable bomb halves found in the spares box, the top ends being removed and the bottoms rounded before they are cemented in place in the top section. Wiring and junction boxes should be fashioned from sprue and plastic card and fixed to the back bulkhead. A certain amount of artistic licence can be used in this compartment as when it is completed the hatch is only three quarters open and held in place by a stay, so merely a suggestion of 'complicated' interior is sufficient. The purist will no doubt shudder at this suggestion and will want to be more precise, this is com-

Above *The crew entry door for the 1:32 scale model. The bar across the window was not fitted to all aircraft. The hinges and entry levers have been fabricated from sprue and white glue.*

Below *The Revell 1:32 scale fuselage with the hatch, bomb-bay and crew entry door removed.*

Bottom *The bomb-bay roof and services hatch compartment in the starboard side of the Revell kit.*

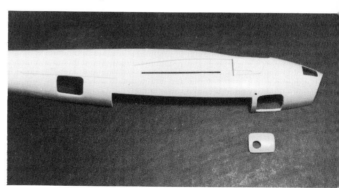

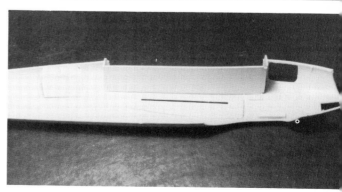

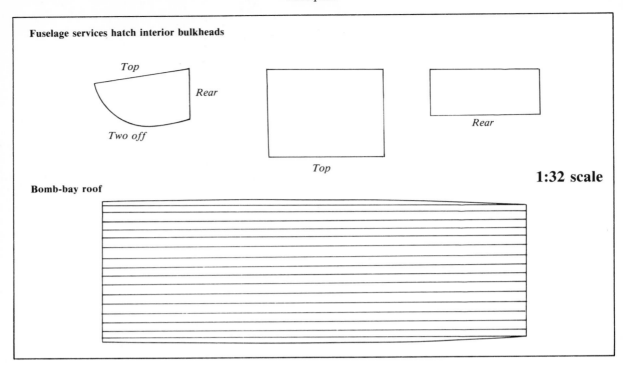

Fuselage services hatch interior bulkheads

Top

Rear

Two off

Top

Rear

1:32 scale

Bomb-bay roof

mendable and should be encouraged, but whatever you do do not open the hatch, make the compartment, then leave it empty.

The most important part of the fuselage interior is the cockpit and this area provides an amazing amount of scope for not-too-difficult detail work. Detail has been engraved on the cockpit side walls but this is best removed as it is shown flat whereas the control boxes and wire runs should be in three dimensions. Cockpit interiors differed from Mark to Mark but a general guide can be obtained from the previously mentioned *Mosquito Manual*, there are also good photographs in *Mosquito at War* and Sharp and Bowyer's definitive work *Mosquito*. Before adding any side consoles, wiring and general detail, concentrate on the instrument panel (part 4). As presented in the kit, the panel is quite good and certainly provides the base from which a good representation can be made. The instructions say to paint it black with white dials, but this is totally inaccurate and should be ignored. A panel can be obtained in the series of photographically reduced ones marketed by Model Accessories Company which were available from AIR Hobbies of Pemberton, New Jersey. These panels are acceptable on a 1:72 scale model where the cockpit area is small, but in 1:32 scale they look far from convincing. I found the best solution was to drill out the instruments etched into the kit panel, using a variety of different-sized drills matched as far as possible to the marked instruments, paint the panel matt black and place it on one side until dry. A piece of .010 in plastic card was cemented to the back face and when

dry trimmed to the exact outline shape of the main panel. When this is done there will be white faces showing through the drilled holes, and these should be filled with gloss black paint. When dry a scriber with a very fine point, or even a sharp needle, is used to mark graduations on the panels by carefully scratching away the gloss paint revealing the original white plastic card. Each instrument then has a drop of gloss varnish dropped in from the front to represent glass. The oil temperature and pressure gauges, as well as the two showing coolant temperature, have yellow bezels and these can easily be added using diluted matt yellow with a very fine brush. This bank of six instruments is located to the port side just forward of the compass. The panel is dry brushed silver which will highlight the dials and instrument rims. To the centre of the panel are located the undercarriage and flap selector levers, these are made from stretched sprue or fuse wire with their control knobs formed from a touch of PVA glue or filler, and painted yellow when dry.

The rudder pedals are the correct shape and moulded to the base of the kit instrument panel, all that is necessary is some refinement with wet-and-dry and thinning down of the side members. If you choose to displace the control surfaces as I did on my model, then to be strictly accurate the pedals should be displaced to align with the position of the rudder. This is going to extremes but the canopy is very clear and such detail work can be seen if it is carried out. The magnetic compass is located on the port side of the cockpit wall just below the instrument panel, and is made from

laminations of plastic card with the graticles and points marked on the top; I fitted mine to a shelf which was cemented to the cockpit wall. Immediately behind the compass can be found the throttle and propeller pitch levers and their associated quadrant. This assembly was made from plastic card and the levers from fuse wire and PVA glue, details being taken from the photographic sources already mentioned. Figures 1, 2, and 3 of Part V in Section Two of the *Mosquito Manual* contain very clear and precise details of the instrument panel and port and starboard side cockpit walls — they are essential study for those who want their model to contain very accurate details. If the entry hatch is opened it is necessary to modify the cockpit floor (part 3) otherwise the hatch will open on to a solid wall of plastic. Before cutting away the area shown on the drawing, it is best to remove the quilting moulded into the observer's seat and replace this with a solid base made from plastic card. Similarly the pilot's seat and the back-rest to the observer's must have the harness details removed and replaced by new ones made either from drafting tape or five thou plastic card. The former has the texture of material and when painted in olive drab and fitted with fuse wire buckles looks very good. I cut out the slot in the back of the pilot's seat where the

moulded harness is attached, then threaded the new harness through this and anchored it in the lower fuselage. Once this work has been done the floor area can be cut away and the edges cleaned up. Fitting of the instrument panels, control column and other equipment to the floor can now be completed and the assembly fitted into the fuselage half. Before doing this it is wise to paint the complete interior of both fuselage halves, the new bomb-bay bulkheads, the interior of the equipment hatch and the cockpit: use Humbrol Interior Green HD 1. Do not try to skimp on the interior painting, since with the hatches open it is easy to see untreated plastic, the best way to ensure that this does not happen is to paint the complete fuselage interior. The instrument panel and various 'boxes' in the cockpit area, are painted matt black, which is highlighted by judicious dry brushing with silver and steel. But remember the Mosquito was a wooden aircraft and there are areas when worn paint-

Above *The open bomb-bay and crew entry hatch with detail added from stretched sprue are all very apparent in this close-up of the Revell B IV (Ian Jebbett ARPS).*

Right *Drilling out the instruments on the 1:32 scale Revell kit. The drill is held in a pin vice.*

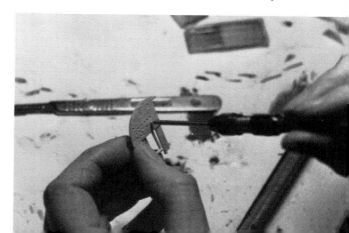

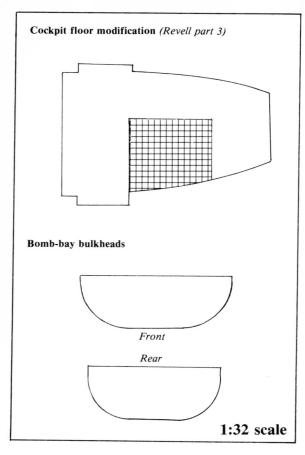

Cockpit floor modification *(Revell part 3)*

Bomb-bay bulkheads

Front

Rear

1:32 scale

Below *The modified cockpit floor for the Revell 1:32 scale kit showing the area of floor which must be removed.*

work would not reveal a silver metal surface. This does not apply to the crew seats, or panels in the cockpit and worn edges to these and scuff marks on rudder panels, add to the air of authenticity.

Ensure that all internal parts are located correctly, then cement the two halves together, not forgetting the tailwheel assembly, and the windows in the nose. The latter are not 100 per cent correct in shape and are slightly oversize; on my model I left them as they were supplied in the kit, but if you want to reduce them the best method is to wait until they are firmly set, then sand them until they are flush with the surrounding area; at the painting stage mask out the correct shape and size and paint around it. My own feelings are that the error in shape is so insignificant that it is hardly worth worrying about.

The front bomb-bay bulkhead satisfactorily blanks off the rear of the cockpit floor, but the front end must be blanked off with a piece of plastic card or filler otherwise it gives an open area in the nose.

When the assembly has set, sand the joins with a medium grade wet-and-dry and while doing this round off the top fuselage section until it is more elliptical. This work will remove the external strengthening ribs which run along the top axis of the fuselage and around its diameter immediately behind the cockpit. The longitudal strengthener is oversize and is hardly missed, but the lateral one is very prominent in most photographs of Mosquitoes and should be retained. Both can be replaced with ten thou Microstrip if you feel particularly strongly about having them. The kit I used had several sink marks and I filled these with Milliput which I find most excellent for this work since it does not flake out in such small areas when it is being worked on.

There are many other areas which can be attended to while the fuselage assembly is setting, and in between major detailing I chose to cut out the control surfaces to give the model a more natural appearance. Having cut the rudder off parts 58 and 59 I encountered a problem which turned out to be common to all such removed flying surfaces; this was the gap left between component halves when they were joined together. This was simply overcome by leaving each component to set, then cementing a strip of ten thou plastic card over the gap, liquid cement was used because when applied with a brush it flows into the whole area to which the plastic strip is fixed. When the strips had set it was a simple matter to trim them to the correct shape and finish off with very fine wet-and-dry paper. After working on the rudder I turned my attention to the elevators, cutting these from parts 54 to 56, sealing the leading edge gaps with plastic card, then sanding smooth. The separated control surfaces were omitted from the model until it was complete and ready for painting and then fixed at realistic angles. The same treatment can be given to ailerons and flaps on the wings, but I chose only to cut the dividing line between the wings and control surfaces and not actually displace them. If you want to separate

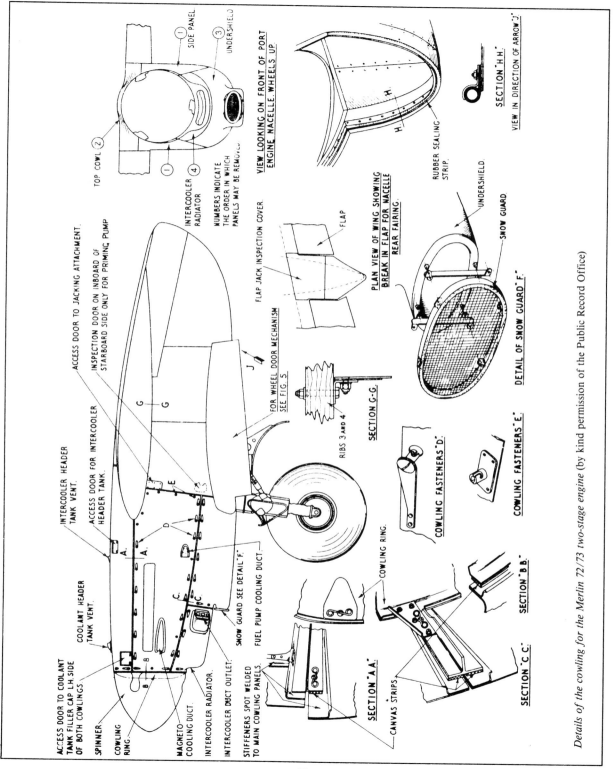

SIDE PANEL

UNDERSHIELD

VIEW LOOKING ON FRONT OF PORT
ENGINE NACELLE. WHEELS UP.

SECTION "H.H."
VIEW IN DIRECTION OF ARROW "J".

TOP COWL

INTERCOOLER
RADIATOR

NUMBERS INDICATE
THE ORDER IN WHICH
THE PANELS MAY BE REMOVED.

FLAP

PLAN VIEW OF WING SHOWING
BREAK IN FLAP FOR NACELLE
REAR FAIRING.

FLAP JACK INSPECTION COVER

RUBBER SEALING
STRIP.

UNDERSHIELD.

SNOW GUARD.

DETAIL OF SNOW GUARD "F."

ACCESS DOOR TO JACKING ATTACHMENT.

INSPECTION DOOR ON INBOARD OF
STARBOARD SIDE ONLY FOR PRIMING PUMP.

FOR WHEEL DOOR MECHANISM
SEE FIG 5

J

G

G

RIBS 3 AND 4

SECTION "G-G."

COWLING FASTENERS "D."

COWLING FASTENERS "E."

ACCESS DOOR TO COOLANT
TANK FILLER CAP L.H. SIDE
OF BOTH COWLINGS.

SPINNER

COWLING
RING.

INTERCOOLER HEADER
TANK VENT.

ACCESS DOOR FOR INTERCOOLER
HEADER TANK.

COOLANT HEADER
TANK VENT.

MAGNETO
COOLING DUCT.

INTERCOOLER RADIATOR.

INTERCOOLER DUCT OUTLET.

STIFFENERS SPOT WELDED
TO MAIN COWLING PANELS.

SNOW GUARD SEE DETAIL "F."

FUEL PUMP COOLING DUCT.

A

A

B

B

C

C

D

E

COWLING RING.

SECTION "AA."

CANVAS STRIPS.

SECTION "C.C."

SECTION "B.B."

Details of the cowling for the Merlin 72/73 two-stage engine (by kind permission of the Public Record Office)

89

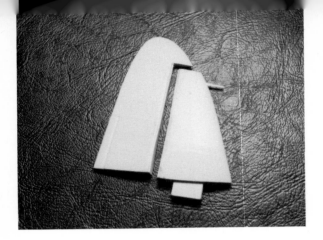

the ailerons remember that they work in opposition, so when you fit them back to the wing, if port is down, starboard will be up and vice versa.

The Revell kit comes with a Merlin engine and exposed nacelle on the port side, the panel has been moulded very accurately so if you do not want to show the engine this can be cemented in the closed position. However, if the model is to be used in a diorama the exposed engine presents a tremendous number of variations for the scene which is to be depicted.

The engine itself comprises just six parts, but details of the Merlin installation are not too difficult to come by and it is not hard to add additional detail from plastic card, sprue, fuse wire and other odds and ends. Once again the *Mosquito Manual* is invaluable and figures 4 to 8 and 12 in Section Five will prove invaluable. It is worthwhile drilling out the exhaust stubs especially if the shrouds, parts 64 to 67, are to be omitted; should you decide to do this remember to fill the locating holes in the nacelle into which the exhaust shrouds locate.

Engine bearers can be made from plastic strip and added around the Merlin before it is finally installed, but care must be taken not to overdo the structure otherwise problems in locating all the additional detail into the engine nacelle might be experienced. Before getting to this stage, paint the interior of the nacelles, including the parts moulded to the top wing sections. The wing radiators can be improved by filing the detail off the fronts of parts 25, and covering these with a fine gauze which can either be part of a pair of discarded tights, or a bandage cemented to the plastic with liquid cement. Before fixing the top and bottom sections of the wings together, paint the area above the landing lights with a mixture of silver and steel, or better still, cement a piece of cooking foil, dull side out, to this area, this will suitably simulate the reflectors and is much better than plain moulded plastic. Cement the wing sections together, assemble the engine nacelles to them, but omit the undercarriage installation as this will hinder important work which *must* be carried out. This work is needed to correct what is perhaps the most serious error on the kit.

If a cross-section of the rear engine nacelle is taken it will be found that it is bi-concave, whereas on the kit the nacelle walls are parallel. The cross-section is important if the model is to capture the true feel of the original and it is not difficult to correct the kit, although the work needed is laborious and cannot be rushed.

When the nacelles are set, apply a thin layer of Milliput to the rear ends of both sides of each nacelle, and follow this with successive layers gradually building up the concave curves either side. Do not rush this work and do not try to use one large portion of Milliput moulded into shape with the fingers, this appears to work but I found the volume too great to produce the adhesion to the plastic which I felt was necessary. As the layers are built-up the shape is gradually developed, and as the last layers are applied it is possible to wet the fingers and smooth the Milliput to a flat surface which then needs little work with wet-and-dry. During this operation filler is also used to provide a better join between the nacelle and wing surfaces, as well as improving the bottom line of the carburettor intake. It is vital that the Milliput is left to set really hard before it is finally smoothed with a very fine grade wet-and-dry, after which it is advisable to apply a thin coat of grey paint which will quickly show any areas where small chips, holes, or scratches, require additional sanding or filling.

The whole rear end of the nacelle now takes on a completely new appearance and when compared with a model which has not had this work carried out, the difference is quite outstanding.

Work can now be carried out on the undercarriage and this can present problems to the fastidious modeller who is looking for absolute accuracy. The first problem, which is not too hard to overcome, is that the legs are a shade too long and make the model sit too high. I removed 3 mm from each leg which, of course, included the locating pins, but I opened the locating holes to accept the shorter legs and fitted them with epoxy glue instead of polystyrene, and a much stronger join seems to have resulted.

The main legs are a trifle too narrow in cross section but it is hard to correct this as retraction jacks, and door guides are moulded to them. At the end of the day it is probably wise to compromise by leaving them as they are and being satisfied with just the shortening of the legs.

There are minor changes to the undercarriage

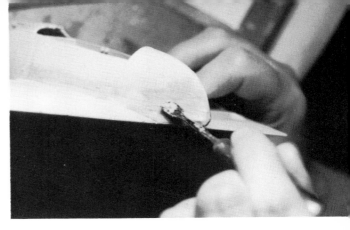

Far left Control surfaces were separated on the Revell 1:32 scale model to produce a more candid appearance, this is typical of the work needed and shows the rudder separated from the fin.

Right The engine nacelles on the Revell 1:32 scale kit are totally incorrect at the rear end, they must be built-up and sanded to the correct shape with Milliput or some other similar filler.

Below Profile of the B IV showing the detailed wheel hubs and mudguards. The pitot head on the fin should be slightly longer but was broken off in the photographic session (Ian Jebbett ARPS).

assemblies on many Mosquito Marks, but it is hard to pin-point these and if major conversions are going to be carried out using the Revell 1:32 kit, the modeller is very much on his own and must decide whether or not he is going to ferret out the details and how best to modify the kit parts; the only real answer as far as the latter is concerned is to scratch-build. The wheels also present a similar problem, they are fine for the prototype and some early aircraft, but later models had different treads and hubs. These problems are not that hard to solve as the ever faithfull Milliput can be used to fill the treads and slots in the hubs, then new treads have to be cut. Another solution would be to use the wheels as masters from which resin ones could be moulded using the now popular cold rubber mould method.

When assembling the kit undercarriage to the wheel wells make sure that each set of legs is parallel to the other and located properly, otherwise the model will develop a list either to port or starboard. The Revell kit has some detail included in the wheel wells but this can be enhanced by the careful use of sprue and plastic card to add additional detail to the interior as well as the undercarriage doors. Before final assembly of the undercarriage members it is advisable carefully to thin down the mudguards, parts 34, as these are a little on the heavy side. The two intake screens, parts 47, can be improved in the same way as the radiators were, by

sanding off the scribed screen detail and replacing it with gauze from a bandage.

Paint the insides of the spinners, parts 73, matt black, and sand the propeller blades to a finer cross-section before adding them to their locating plates, parts 69/71. Before fixing the spinners, paint the propeller hubs with a mix of steel and dark grey, then dry brush silver around the reduction gear. It is best to omit the propeller assemblies until the model has been completely finished, and painted accordingly before being married to the rest of the airframe.

The final major task before painting and adding aerials, weathering and markings, is the cockpit canopy.

The canopy in the kit is a beautiful clear moulding which assembles perfectly but it is too deep. The only real solution is to mould a completely new canopy but this does present problems to all but the very skilled, since observation blisters are moulded integrally and must be made as separate items on any home-built replacement. As the expert modeller will probably not require any advice on moulding or forming a new canopy, attention must be given to the less experienced or those without the expertise needed. If the depth of the canopy is reduced by careful sanding of the base-line, it will not then fit the fuselage recess unless the size of this is made to match by the addition of a plastic card skirt inserted into the existing cockpit shell. There are two far

easier alternatives, one is to accept the fault and live with it; this is not really a coward's way out since if the rest of the model is made as described the canopy does not look too obtrusive. The second is to fit the canopy in place, then change the lower line with a thin coat of filler which is sanded into the cockpit contours then painted as part of the fuselage. This is a task which needs extremely careful work and does result in the loss of some canopy detailing. Summing up, my personal view is that if you feel you are not competent to mould a new canopy, live with the one provided in the kit.

The decals (transfers) provided in the kit are for DZ353 GB:E of 105 Squadron RAF and are very basic in their content, consisting of the national marking in which the yellow of the fuselage roundels is too pale, squadron codes, aircraft letter, serial and W/T bonding points. In this scale it is not easy to find alternatives but, on the other hand, the spares box is likely to produce roundels of the correct size and individual codes can either be hand painted or cut from solid colour sheets. It is not hard to cut stencils from Fisk masking tape and this material can be successfully used to make national markings as described in my book *Making Model Aircraft*.

There seems to be little point in detailing painting methods and schemes as, in the case of the former, every modeller has his own pet methods, whether he uses brushes or an air-brush, and the latter are readily available in a variety of reference books.

As mentioned earlier in this chapter, the Revell 1:32 scale kit can be used as the basis for many Mosquito conversions; clearly space is not available to describe all these in detail but it is worthwhile mentioning some of the points to look out for in some of the more readily available conversion subjects.

On fighter models the canopy must be modified to have a flat windscreen; this is fairly easy to do, all that is needed being the cutting off of the pointed screen and replacement by a flat one made from acetate or transparent plastic card. The fighter version solid nose can be made by either covering the existing transparent cone with filler, or cutting off the nose using the Airfix kit as a guide, and adding a new nose from wood or moulded plastic card. This would also apply to the radar-nosed night fighters. In all cases where the fighter canopy and nose is fitted, the cockpit opening in the fuselage will need its front end modified to accept the flat-screened canopy, and the control yoke replaced by a single stick

type. On some variants the propeller blades will need to be replaced by scratch-built paddle types, once again the general shape and proportions can be judged from the Airfix kit, and some aircraft will need to have their carburettor intakes lengthened. On aircraft where the six exhaust stubs are shown exposed, the Revell five-stub will have to be modified, but the shape of the sixth stub can be based on the first four moulded on the manifold supplied. The Revell moulding can be used to cast copies in cold rubber and then mould them in resin, cutting off the additional stacks needed and adding them to the kit stacks.

Modelling versions with the two-stage Merlins mean that extensive work is needed on the kit engines, this is not impossible or that difficult. The first step is to cut off the nacelles at the firewall and add a section six scale inches in length using plastic card built up with Milliput then re-attach the part removed. When this assembly is thoroughly set, add the chin inter-cooler intake and extend the carburettor intake with plastic card and Milliput, then sand the whole assembly to the correct shape. Details of the two-stage engine are shown in the drawings and the method used to modify the 1:72 scale Airfix engines can be equally successfully used in this larger scale.

The bulged bomb-bay used on bomber and later PR versions is just an exercise in adding a balsa block and carving to shape, or carving the shape from a harder wood and using this in the evergreen male and female moulding method. Some PR versions had strengthening external stringers on both fuselage sides, and camera ports varied from Mark to Mark, so checking against photographs, drawings and other reference material is essential. Finally do not forget that that fighter versions had the entry door moved to the fuselage side as the nose armament occupied the space under the cockpit floor, and some late Mark bomber and PR versions had an additional blister on top of the canopy.

The challenge in modifying the Revell kit is an exciting one, study of available reference material, careful thought of the best way to tackle the work, some of the detailing and tips given here, will provide the recipe for many hours of modelling pleasure, which is only likely to be curtailed by the cost factor and, perhaps more important, the lack of available display space. So if you are a Mosquito enthusiast, think carefully about your favourite version then tackle the Revell kit, the result will be well worthwhile.

Chapter Nine

Conversions

The prototype Mosquito

The graceful lines of the Mosquito changed very little throughout its development, it is not therefore too difficult to produce any version from the kits available irrespective of scale. The amount of work involved will, of course, depend a great deal on the choice of scale; those selecting the 1:32 scale Mosquito described in the last chapter face a considerable amount of work, while at the other end of the spectrum, the popular 1:72 scale kits provide a considerable amount of 'raw' material.

Most of the conversions described in this, and the following, chapter can be created from any kit, since it does not require a great deal of thought to apply the same principles and changes to any scale. Similarly the methods used can also vary to suit the modeller concerned, all I have attempted to do is to lay the foundations from which the particular Mosquito described can be constructed. It is not possible in the space available to describe every possible conversion, but it is a simple matter to cross-reference those selected to versions derived from them, and incorporate the same modifications plus any others needed to produce any variant within a Mark.

The Monogram 1:48 scale kit seemed to be an ideal choice for making a model of the prototype Mosquito since, as already described, there are a number of points needing attention and while these were being worked on

the additional conversion work could also be carried out.

The general comments made in the description of the Monogram kit should be re-read and a decision taken as to just how far you propose to go in correcting the errors described. For the purpose of this chapter and to keep the work involved within the reach of every modeller, I chose to leave the fuselage in its original form since to improve its cross-sectional area shape only leads to increasing problems. I also felt that, as the Monogram model was only being used as a typical example, it was essential to keep the work roughly within the parameters of that needed to make a prototype from any kit.

The clear-nosed bomber fuselage is the one needed for the prototype Mosquito so parts G1 and G2 are used as they come in the kit. Before cementing the two halves together it is advisable to remove the fin/rudder along the base-line where it joins the fuselage. This work is essential on the Monogram kit as this component is approximately 5 mm too tall. Having removed the fin/rudder there are two choices open, one is to reduce the height of the kit-moulded component and change the leading edge shape, the other is to build a completely new part from plastic card. If the latter course is followed it is necessary to simulate the fabric-covered rudder by first cementing strips of .010 in plastic card to represent the ribbing. When these are dry, lightly sand them to reduce their prominence, then paint liquid

The first prototype. It was yellow over-all with black spinners, codes and radio mast. The top wing roundels were Type B.

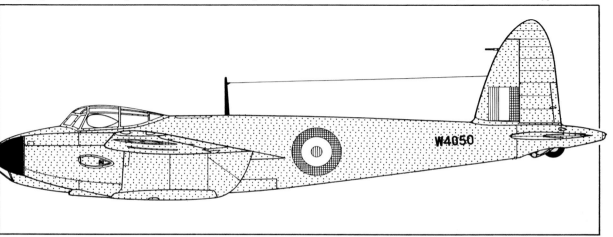

Above *The Monogram 1:48 scale kit modified to the all-yellow prototype. Wing leading edge slots and exhaust system are very noticeable additions* (Ian Jebbett ARPS).

Left *Plan view of the prototype showing the revised rear ends of the engine cowlings which do not break the line of the wing trailing edges. The leading edge slots are also very apparent* (Ian Jebbett ARPS).

Below *Rear ends of the engine nacelles require considerable work to change the outline shape for the prototype aircraft. The aerial mast is black and lost in the background* (Ian Jebbett ARPS).

Above right *The elevator hinge actuator cover which was on all Mosquitoes but is shown in a variety of sizes and positions in most kits. This is the prototype at Salisbury Hall.*

Above far right *The Monogram 1:48 scale kit being modified into the prototype Mosquito. The rear engine nacelle fairing has been removed giving a totally unbroken wing trailing edge.*

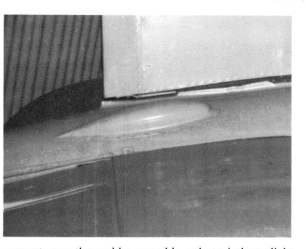

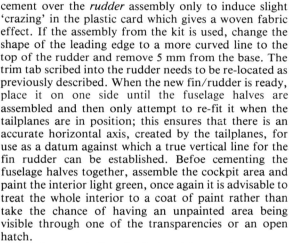

cement over the *rudder* assembly only to induce slight 'crazing' in the plastic card which gives a woven fabric effect. If the assembly from the kit is used, change the shape of the leading edge to a more curved line to the top of the rudder and remove 5 mm from the base. The trim tab scribed into the rudder needs to be re-located as previously described. When the new fin/rudder is ready, place it on one side until the fuselage halves are assembled and then only attempt to re-fit it when the tailplanes are in position; this ensures that there is an accurate horizontal axis, created by the tailplanes, for use as a datum against which a true vertical line for the fin rudder can be established. Befoe cementing the fuselage halves together, assemble the cockpit area and paint the interior light green, once again it is advisable to treat the whole interior to a coat of paint rather than take the chance of having an unpainted area being visible through one of the transparencies or an open hatch.

The circular windows in the bomb bay and crew entry hatch are missing from the kit so these must be added, as described for the Revell kit in the last chapter

With tailplanes and the fin/rudder in place the fuselage assembly can be left to set while the major work for this particular conversion is carried out; this being the modifications of the wings and engine nacelles.

The prototype Mosquito had short engine nacelles which did not break the line of the wing trailing edge; a feature also applicable to the first ten production versions, thus opening alternative conversion possibilities for those who perhaps have only operational aircraft in their collections.

The wingspan of the first Mosquito was 52 ft 6 in whereas that in the versions represented by the Monogram — and most other kits — was 54 ft 2 in so a scale 1 ft 8 in which is .416 in in 1:48 and .278 in in 1:72 has to be removed. In my view the best time to do this is after the wing halves have been put together and the work on the engine nacelles completed.

Before cementing the wing halves together, cut off the pointed rear end engine nacelle fairings which are

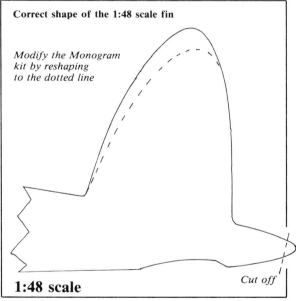

Correct shape of the 1:48 scale fin

Modify the Monogram kit by reshaping to the dotted line

Cut off

1:48 scale

moulded to the trailing edges of the top wing sections, parts G26 and G27. The kit instructions advise the modeller to place the completed undercarriage assembly into the engine nacelles before cementing the wing halves together, if this is done the undercarriage presents a considerable handicap when the extensive surgery, filling and sanding are being carried out. I found it best to ignore this instruction and simply cement parts G4, G5, G26 and G27 together after first fitting the landing light lenses in position and simulating their reflectors with silver foil in the correct position above them in parts G26/27, this simulation can, of course, also be effected with silver paint. Once the work on the engine nacelles is completed the task of locating the undercarriage is a difficult one requiring a lot of hit-and-miss fiddling until it is in place. It is best to tackle this work with 'dry' components and once they are

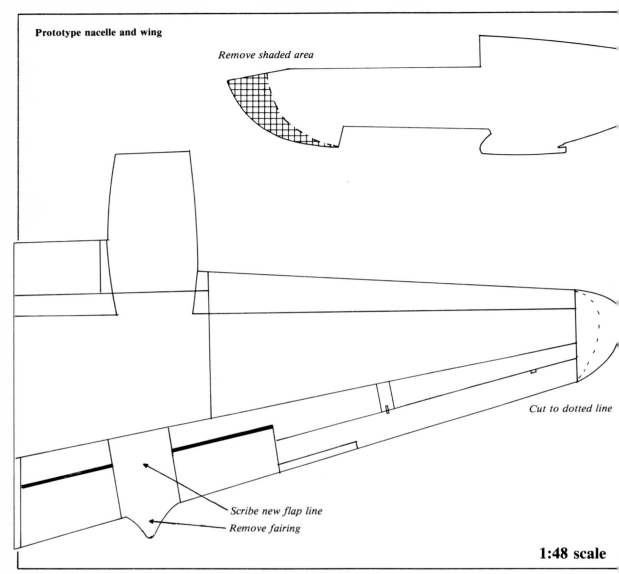

Prototype nacelle and wing

Remove shaded area

Cut to dotted line

Scribe new flap line

Remove fairing

1:48 scale

correctly located apply a mix of liquid and tube cement with a paint brush. The alternative is to follow the laid down procedure but in doing this frustration is almost certain to arise as the modification work is undertaken.

When the components have set, take a razor saw and make a cut 1 mm aft of the rear undercarriage door line at an angle of approximately 30 degrees to the vertical line scribed on the nacelle at this point. This cut stops just short of the lower wing surface, then a modelling knife with a sharp blade is used to make a cut parallel to the wing surfaces and out to the nacelle trailing edge. A profile of the new rear end to the engine nacelle was cut from 20 thou plastic card and cemented vertically into the space created by the removal of the moulding. The new shape was then built up with Milliput, this being

smoothed into the correct contours with a wet finger before it finally set, after which it was rubbed down with progressively finer grades of wet-and-dry. Whilst the Milliput was in its 'ready' condition, it was also used to fill the two scribed lines on the top wing surfaces which bisect the flaps at the point where the engine nacelle fairing was removed. This area was also sanded smooth when the filler had dried and a new area of flap hinge line was scribed in, giving a new continuous line parallel to the trailing edge. The exhaust stack shrouds, parts G32-G35, are not needed for this version as the cowling in the area where they fit was perfectly smooth, so it is a simple matter to fill the locating holes and sand smooth. The prototype's exhaust system comprises outlets just forward and below the wing leading edges, so these must be fabricated from sprue and cemented in place. Some of the early aircraft which had the short engine nacelles, had variations in exhaust systems, so it is advisable to check reference material relating to the particular model chosen as the conversion subject. In *Profile Publication No 52* there is a good source of photographic reference for the prototype NF II, W4052 showing its exhaust layout, and on page 7 there are several photographs of PR versions, including the prototype, W4051, which show to advantage the variations in exhaust systems as well as the rear end shape of the short nacelle. Handley-Page slots were fitted to the wing leading edges of W4050 but they were found to be unnecessary and were not used or fitted to production aircraft. The slots were covered with fabric and can still be seen on the aircraft which forms part of the display in the Mosquito Museum at Salisbury Hall, although any modeller using this as a reference source should be aware that the aircraft as it stands today, is *not* as it was when it made its maiden flight. The slots are represented by 6 cm strips of ten thou plastic card cemented to the leading edges outboard of the engine nacelles, the extreme end of the slot being located 2 mm from the line scribed at the wing tip.

When the work on the engine nacelles has been completed the span is reduced by the amounts mentioned earlier, this is done by careful sanding at the wing tips remembering to retain the over-all shape, but at the same time keeping in mind that the navigation and formation lights will have to be re-positioned.

The pointed windscreen cockpit, parts C39 and C40, is used and fitted after all assembly has been carried out, it now only remains to clean-up the whole airframe with a light grade wet-and-dry, re-scribe panel lines where necessary and prepare the model for painting.

To aid aircraft recognition the prototype was originally painted over-all yellow with black spinners and A type roundels in six positions (both fuselage sides, the top and lower wing surfaces). For the first two test flights the B condition serial E-0234 was applied to the rear fuselage but this was then changed to W4050. Markings can be obtained from the spares box with the serial coming from Letraset or one of the Modeldecal sheets which contains a selection of various sized black numbers and letters.

The correct shade of yellow to use is rather evasive, some of those who saw the original claim that the present colour used at Salisbury Hall is too dark, whilst others say it is too light and yet others maintain it is just right! So again there is the old colour controversy, I would not presume to know the correct colour to use but a consensus suggests that Humbrol Matt Yellow (No 24), slightly darkened, is about right.

For those modellers who like constructing dioramas the prototype Mosquito gives plenty of opportunity to create scenes which are different from the usual war-like settings favoured by many. Most books about the aircraft contain a selection of photographs of the first Mosquito undergoing tests before it actually flew. In such scenes parts of it are covered with tarpaulins, wheel

Above *The rear section of the Monogram engine nacelle has been removed ready for reshaping with filler and scrap plastic.*

Below *The rear end of the engine nacelle of the Monogram kit has now been reshaped to the line of the original prototype which did not break the trailing edge.*

Bottom *Useful undercarriage detail on the prototype as it now is at Salisbury Hall.*

Above left *W4050 the all-yellow prototype being readied for its first flight. The bottom sections of the cowlings have been removed and the undercarriage doors are not yet fitted (BAeC).*

Above right *The second prototype W4051. Compare this with the previous picture and note the many subtle differences such as the exhaust arrangement and oleo legs (BAeC).*

Below *Interesting nose art on an Australian Mosquito (MoD).*

doors are missing, and there is a lot of equipment laying around, one particular shot also shows a pre-war saloon car; a real challenge for the scratch-builder!

Miscellaneous Mosquitoes

Modellers who have chosen 1:72 scale — and evidence still suggests that this is the most popular for aircraft modelling — have a variety of ready-made subjects in the Airfix and Matchbox kits of the Mosquito. Combining parts from these kits does eliminate some scratch-building or modification, but on the other side of the coin such combinations result in necessary compromise, minor changes to components and, of course, double expenditure. As with most hobbies expenditure must be put into the correct perspective right from the start, and there are two ways of looking at this as far as the Mosquito is concerned. The impecunious modeller will no doubt select one kit and from this derive the conver-

sions he wants by modifying component parts, in this respect the choice is likely to be the Matchbox offering for it is slightly less expensive than the Airfix kit. Having said that, at the other end of the scale is the modeller who perhaps does not have such a strict budget and is able to buy several of each kit available and cross-match the parts he wants; it is also possible that the less skilled modeller might well be tempted by the latter especially if he feels that making new engine nacelles, for example, is beyond his abilities. It is not for me to say which approach is best, so I have attempted to steer a middle course by showing how it is possible to cross-match, but have also covered certain modifications in ways which apply to either kit. The decision as to which method is used rests entirely with the reader who, after all, knows the depth of his own pocket and the limits of his modelling skills.

There can be no doubt that the Airfix kit is superior, in that all-important ingredient of finesse, to the Matchbox offering but it must be remembered that it is more expensive and, as with everything in life, one only gets what one pays for. The Matchbox model lacks a certain amount of surface detailing such as panel lines and the bomb-bay demarcation lines; these, however, are not beyond the skill of even the tyro and a sharp-pointed modelling knife or scriber soon corrects this deficiency.

It is gratifying that the two manufacturers produced entirely different aircraft, since the two-stage Merlins in the Matchbox kit certainly help to overcome one of the problems in converting the Airfix kit to versions using this power plant.

Before going on to look at specific conversions, it would seem worthwhile taking a look at components which can be cross-matched, and sorting out the problems arising.

The kit designers concerned have approached the subject in entirely different ways and this does make

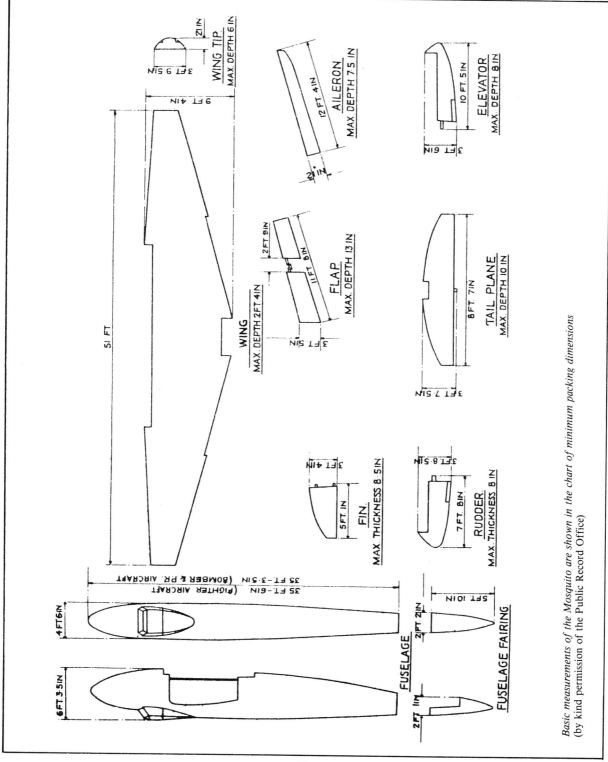

Basic measurements of the Mosquito are shown in the chart of minimum packing dimensions (by kind permission of the Public Record Office)

Looking for something a little unusual; then how about this Nationalist Chinese aircraft? (George Stewart via Stuart Howe).

changes difficult in some areas. Perhaps the most important feature, as far as the serious conversion addict is concerned, is the interchangeability of the power plants. Airfix have chosen to mould the total top cowling as an integral part of the top wing surface, whereas Matchbox have cut off the cowling just forward of the leading edge. Major surgery is necessary to adapt either wing to take the other's engine nacelle; the easy way out is completely to interchange the whole wing assembly between the two models. To do this it is necessary to modify the locating tongues and slots on both fuselages, but this work is of a very minor nature, the result is that the two-stage Matchbox wing can be fitted to the Airfix fuselage and vice versa. This means, for example, that a clear-nosed Mk IV bomber can be produced in two ways, one by fitting the Airfix wing and engine assemblies to the Matchbox fuselage on which alternative nose section 29, 30 and 31, has been fitted, or the latter nose section can be fitted to the Airfix kit. Fortunately the Matchbox fuselage has been moulded without any nose forward of the wing leading edges at the root, the alternative noses provided cementing to this area when the choice has been made. Although this results in the use of filler to obtain the smooth line of the Mosquito nose, it gives a tremendous advantage as both the alternate nose sections can be fitted to the Airfix fuselage with only minor adjustments. If the Airfix fuselage nose is cut off the Matchbox alternatives fit with only a minor amount of filler being required, but it is worth stressing that the cuts made must be accurate and parallel to each other or matching will be difficult.

Changing the nose areas in this way does result in work on the cockpit base line as the canopies from each kit only fit precisely to their own fuselages. If the clear bomber nose is added to the Airfix kit then the match-box pointed windscreen canopy, part 26, must be used and the rear end of this where it is required to match the Airfix fuselage needs some careful sanding to change its contours. Similarly if the bulbous radar nose, part 27/28, is fitted to the Airfix kit then the Airfix canopy,

part 68, will need changing at its front end or the Matchbox canopy, part 24, will need attention to its rear end. It is worth repeating that the location of crew entry hatches must be carried out with some care, bomber versions had a hatch under the nose, whereas fighters had a side door as scribed in the Airfix kit. If the latter is modified to a glazed-nose bomber then the scribed door must be removed, if the change is carried out by using a Matchbox nose then the door will disappear during surgery. As Matchbox have failed to mark either entry, the problem is an academic one as it has to be added in either case.

There are other components which can be exchanged and perhaps the most obvious being those which go together to make the undercarriage. If the Matchbox wing assemblies are used on the Airfix fuselage it is obviously easier to use the Matchbox landing gear, but this lacks the detail of the Airfix offering so the really fastidious modeller has two choices; one, to carry out the complicated work in matching the Airfix under-carriage to the Matchbox wing or, two, to add detail to the Matchbox gear basing this on that included on the Airfix mouldings.

In the following descriptions where scratch-built parts are described this has been done to illustrate how these can be made, but if similar parts are available in the Matchbox kit then they can be used at the discretion of the modeller concerned. All the following conversions are based primarily on the Airfix kit unless otherwise stated.

The Mosquito T III

One full-sized Mosquito which is readily available for close examination by any modeller is the all-silver T III (TW117) displayed at the RAF Museum, Hendon, as this varies very little externally from the NF II it is a very simple conversion on which to start.

The fuselage is assembled as for the Mk II but the nose guns, parts 18, are omitted as their muzzles cannot be seen through the apertures on the Hendon aircraft.

100

The Airfix 1:72 scale kit modified to an RAF T III trainer (Ian Jebbett ARPS).

The underwing surfaces are perfectly clean so it is not necessary to open any of the holes or use any of the underwing stores, so all these parts, together with the discarded nose armament and radar, can be consigned to the spares box. The aircraft at Hendon is fitted with paddle blades so components 29 and 51 will be needed and the pointed blades can take their place alongside the other parts which are not needed. Carry out assembly in the order laid down in the instructions adding interior detail as required, remembering that cockpit detail will be fairly clear through the kit canopy. The latter component is one which has been criticised by some reviewers not because of its shape but because moulding techniques do not give it the same crispness as the rest of the kit parts. Writing in *Scale Models* some time ago, noted modeller Clive Hall spotlighted the problem as the curved interior edges which tend to give the canopy a heavy look. The only satisfactory remedy is to mould a new one and the best way to do this is to use the kit canopy as the master for forming a vac-form replacement on a Mattel tool. Very few British modellers have

this very useful piece of equipment so it is probably best, unless you trust yourself to make a new canopy by the old method of male and female moulding, to live with that supplied in the kit which is generally acceptable, unless you are very hard to please or a 'pot hunter'.

The appearance of the undercarriage can be improved by drilling three small holes on the strengthening web of the mudguard, parts 36 and 58, but to do this a very small dental drill is required and if you do not possess one three dabs of black paint will do just as well. By the way, this attention to detail is worth carrying out on all versions as it is not solely confined to the T III. The only other modification needed is the addition of the small fairing on the starboard fuselage half below the wing root. This is made from a small piece of sprue which is cemented to the fuselage then shaped in situ. Once the wings have set and before they are fixed to the fuselage, cut out a slot in the leading edge of the starboard wing outboard of the engine nacelle and cement into this a scrap of clear plastic cut from a discarded stand. When it has set, sand it into the

A pair of T IIIs in over-all silver finish in service post-war with the RAF (MoD).

Left Early stages in the construction of the T III using the Airfix kit, the dark areas show where filler has been used to improve the shape and smoothness of the original mouldings.

Below A Mosquito T III of 3 CAACU at Exeter. It is silver over-all with yellow trainer bands.

Right T III trainer of the Turkish Air Force; it is silver over-all.

Below right The over-all silver finish and yellow trainer bands offer an interesting alternative scheme for the Airfix kit. This aircraft is the T III in the RAF Museum at Hendon (Ian Jebbett ARPS).

contours of the wing then polish with toothpaste to restore the lustre to what is the transparency of an additional landing light. It only remains to fit the open five-stack exhaust stubs and paint the model in order to add a trainer to the Mosquito collection. This aircraft is painted over-all silver which is a colour which always seems to cause modellers problems. An over-all aluminium sprayed from an air-brush or spray-can always makes any model look unreal, yet hand painting in so many cases seems to result in an equally unimpressive streaky finish. The answer, in my opinion, is to spray silver on to a grey undercoat but change the tone of the colour by mixing varying quantities of steel and light grey to the basic silver. This method does result in the necessity of cutting paper masks for different panels and spraying through these — masking tape applied direct to silver will only spoil the surface. As far as this particular model is concerned, it is best to spray the areas where the trainer bands are to be located first, then cut strips of masking tape to the widths required for the yellow bands and mask out the necessary areas.

Now apply a coat of matt light grey and when this is thoroughly dry, re-spray with a 50/50 mix of silver and light grey. Cut paper masks from writing paper and hold these in position by hand whilst a 30/70 mix is applied, then select other areas for masking and spraying with a 20/80 mix of silver and steel. If this work is carried out carefully and each coat is allowed to dry the result will be an overall aluminium finish with varying tonal areas.

Mosquito night fighters

The Mk II night fighter depicted in the Airfix kit is easily converted to the Mk XII which was the first version to carry centimetric radar and introduce the spinning-dish scanner mounted in the nose. This is a very simple conversion requiring only the fitting of a thimble nose and aerials. The fuselage is assembled as detailed in the kit instructions but part 19 is omitted, the ridge to which this fits is filed flat to form the base for the new nose. The latter can be produced in many different ways, one of the most straightforward is to insert a balsa plug and, when this has set, carve and sand it to the correct shape.

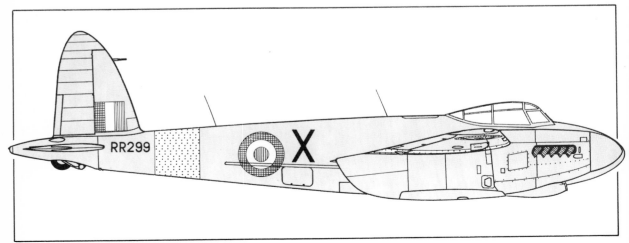

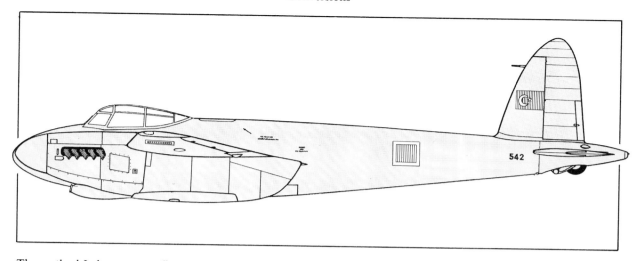

The method I chose was to fit a ten thou plastic disc to the fuselage nose to provide a good solid key, then to this I attached the spinner from a discarded kit which had found its way into the spares box. Any suitably-sized spinner will do and its use certainly saves a lot of time in carving and filling with grain filler. The particular part I used was marginally oversize but reducing its rear end to match the fuselage contours presented no problems after it had firmly set.

This aircraft was fitted with single-stage Merlin 21 or 23 engines so no work was needed on the kit components. Propellers are the standard bladed types so use parts 28 and 50. The only other additions are the wing aerials which are made from stretched sprue and inserted through holes drilled in the wing surfaces. It is best to fit these after all painting is completed otherwise they will continually be broken, and they can be held firmly in place with a touch of liquid cement or even a dab of the top and lower wing surface paint. Another conversion stemming from the Mk XII is the Mk XIII which is basically the same aircaft, though built to carry

centimetric radar, fitted with 50 Imperial gallon wing tanks which can be obtained from the Matchbox kit and fitted to the Airfix wings in the same positions. The small thimble nose was later superseded by the bulbous one which became known as the Universal and late versions of the Mk XIII can be produced by fitting the nose, parts 27 and 28, from the Matchbox kit to the Airfix fuselage. This is done by cutting the nose off the Airfix fuselage just forward of the wing root and attaching the Matchbox components to it, if the cut is made accurately only a minimum amount of filler is required to hide the join. A camera fairing is attached to the starboard side of the nose this being fashioned from a small piece of sprue which is shaped in situ; incidentally, this addition is also needed if the NF 30 version is built straight from the Matchbox kit.

Both early versions described are fitted with shrouded exhausts and have wing aerials in identical positions, these aerials must also be fitted to the NF 30 version and they are not shown in the Matchbox instructions or artwork. The NF 30 version is improved if it is fitted with

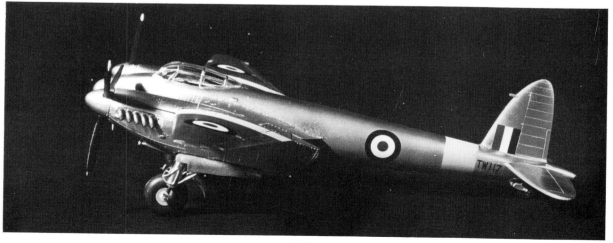

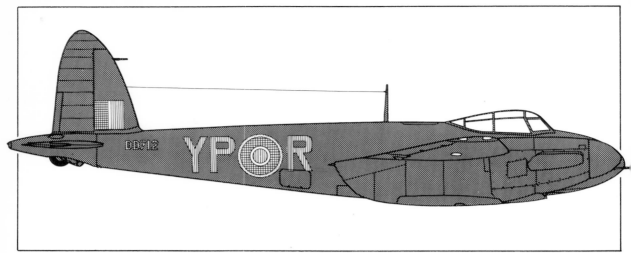

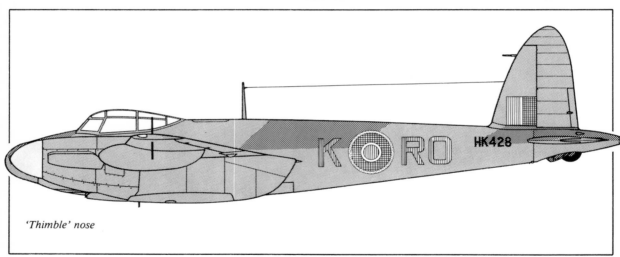

'Thimble' nose

NF XII/XIII radar nose

Drawing courtesy of BAeC

NF 30 nose and engine nacelle

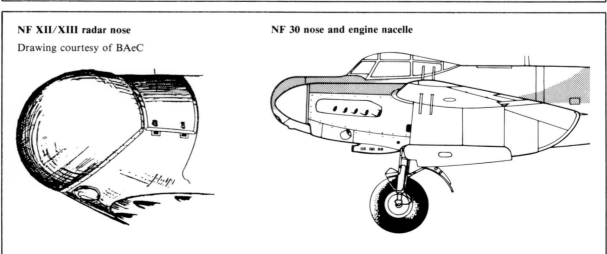

Left *An NF XIII of 29 Squadron RAF. It was Dark Green/Medium Sea Grey with Sky spinners, red codes and a black serial.*
Above far left *An NF II with radar removed, used by 23 Squadron RAF for intruder operations. RDM 2A Night over-all, codes and serial Dull Red.*
Above left *NF XIII conversion using the Airfix kit. The thimble nose is from a discarded spinner.*
Above right *An 85 Squadron NF 30 with paddle blades, wing tip aerials and aircraft's letter S in the squadron hexagon marking on the nose.*

the paddle blades from the Airfix kit as those in the original are not quite broad enough. This interchange is a typical example of spare parts being put to good use, for if either the Mk XII or XIII are converted from the Airfix kit, the paddle blades are not used and can therefore be matched to the Matchbox NF 30. Obviously the NF 30, which was the last night fighter version to be introduced to service in World War 2, can be converted from the Airfix kit either by scratch-building the two-stage Merlin and a bulbous Universal nose, or fitting the Matchbox wings, engines and nose to the Airfix fuselage. The latter is an expensive way of producing a model and it seems more sensible to me to use the Matchbox kit as it comes, but with the addition of the Airfix paddle blades.

For those modellers who want to base all their conversions on the Airfix kit the task of making the deeper, longer two-stage nacelles is not too difficult. One method is to cut off the existing nacelles where they join the wings, insert a balsa plug and carve the new shape; another is to build up the existing components with filler. First take a sharp modelling knife and cut off the small intake moulded to the nacelle, then add layers of Milliput along the bottom line of the nacelle to increase the depth. When this has set firmly, sand it to the correct profile, making sure that the intake is symmetrical about the centre-line. This work must be carried out very carefully with the engine nacelle halves cemented together; thus the addition of a spinning propeller is not too easy, but it can be achieved by locating the pins through the nacelles first, then building up their diameter with Sellotape to prevent them falling back into the nacelle. The Sellotape is removed when the

propellers are cemented into position. Filler can crumble when the chin radiator is gouged out, so to overcome this I fitted sections cut from bomb halves which I again found in the invaluable spares box. The nose ends of the bombs were cut off and the open ended bodies cemented to the base of the nacelles, the filler was then applied around them to achieve the correct shape and, when final work was carried out, the original hard plastic of the bombs enabled a really sharp intake line to be produced. The intakes removed earlier are fitted back into place on the lower line in their new positions and any small gaps resulting are filled. This sounds a lot of unnecessary work when perfectly good engines are available on the Matchbox wing, but there are still some modellers who might find it preferable for reasons of economy or simply a desire to create as much as possible from the original kit parts; the choice is, of course, theirs.

The Mk XIX went into production as an updated version of the Mk XIII but using American radar and the Mk XVII was basically a Mk II but again with American radar equipment. The Universal nose was fitted to all Mk XIXs so yet another version can be added to any collection by selecting the correct squadron markings for a conversion using the Universal nose from the Matchbox kit added to the Airfix fuselage.

The choice of markings and colour schemes is legion and readily available in a variety of listed reference books, so there seems little point in going into specific details within these pages when the space can be better used. One of the most challenging night fighter conversions is the long-span Mk XV; an interesting model

105

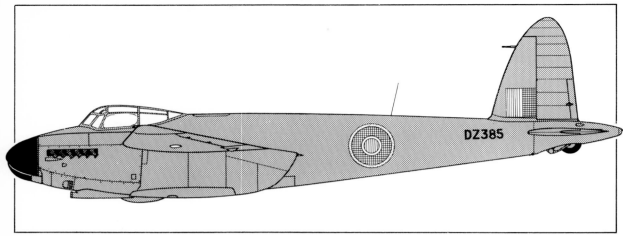

Above *An NF XV high altitude fighter. The colours are Deep Sky over-all with black spinners and radome. Note the bomber-style pointed windscreen.*

Above right *The high altitude Mk XV from the Airfix kit. Note the four-bladed propellers, thimble nose and gun pack. The wind screen should be the pointed type as used on the bomber versions.*

Right *Another view of the Long Span NF XV in its over-all Deep Sky Blue colour scheme.*

Below right *Three quarter head-on view of a Mk XIII of 29 Squadron showing wing aerials and thimble nose.*

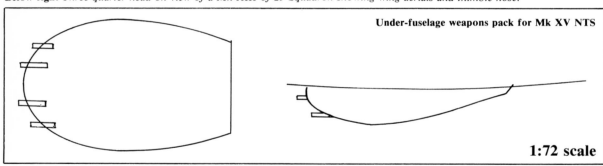

Under-fuselage weapons pack for Mk XV NTS

1:72 scale

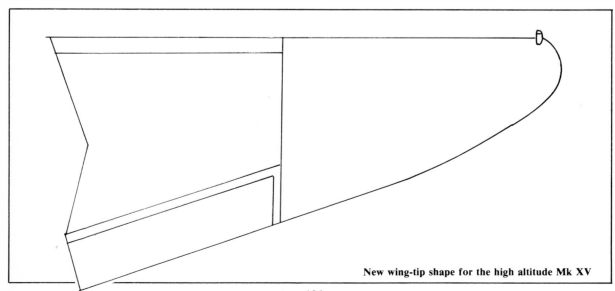

New wing-tip shape for the high altitude Mk XV

both to build and research. There seems to be some controversy as to the exact span of this aircraft, the most often quoted figure is 59 ft 2 in which appears in the definitive work on the aircraft *Mosquito* by Sharp and Bowyer where, on page 396, it is clearly stated that production versions had this dimension. It is also quoted by Birtles and Green in various articles, yet my co-author advises me (despite the comment in his earlier book) that only the prototype MP469 had this span, the other four having theirs increased to 62 ft 7 in.

It seems that the increased span wing was eventually fitted to all five versions including MP469, so for the purpose of this conversion this is the dimension chosen.

The MK XV was fitted with two-stage Merlins so the Matchbox wing/engine assembly must be used if the Airfix kit is to form the basis of the model, it is, however, a simple matter to use the Matchbox kit for this whole conversion, the only addition to the fuselage being a thimble nose as for the Mk XIII. If this option is chosen use parts 29 and 30 for the nose, filling in the window areas with ten thou plastic card and filler first. The thimble is made from a discarded spinner and attached in place of the transparency part 31, being shaped when it is set. The pointed-windscreened canopy, part 26, is required and this must, of course, be used on the Airfix fuselage if this is used instead of the Matchbox one. The blister on the canopy roof must be carefully removed and the area it is taken from restored to its original lustre with fine wet-and-dry and tooth-paste.

The major work is to the wings which must be increased to a total of 10.43 in in span, this is done by cutting off the tips just outboard of the ailerons and adding laminations of plastic card which, to give a better join, can be slotted into the gaps left between the top and bottom sections when the tips are removed. The drawing clearly shows the shape of the revised tips and it is emphasised that no attempt should be made to carry out this shaping until the additions are set hard. The total area of adhesion is very small so work carefully and do not handle the model by the tips once it has been completed.

The engines are fitted with four-bladed propellers which have the normal blades as parts 28 and 50 in the Airfix kit. The spinners in the Airfix kit have a more correct pointed shape so it is best to use these and, it is hoped, if paddle-bladed versions have been constructed sufficient standard propeller blades will be available. Remove the blades from the bosses keeping the angle as constant as possible on each cut. Fill each spinner with Milliput ensuring that the three slots at 120 degrees are completely filled. When this is dry, sand the exterior smooth, then drill four holes at 0 degrees, 90 degrees, 180 degrees and 270 degrees and with the point of a No 11 blade elongate these holes into slots.

Cement the four blades into position making sure that the pitch angle is correct by comparing positions with those on other models or 'undoctored' blades from the kit.

The next task is to make the belly armament pack which was fitted under the fuselage to the rear of the normal armament position. First fill the gun troughs on the fuselage and the bomb-bay lines, if using the Airfix kit, then add the blister by building up three layers of 20 thou plastic card which is shaped in position. When the final shape has been achieved a coat of Milliput is applied and is rubbed smooth once it has set. The gun barrels protrude from the pack and are fabricated from sprue.

The final construction task is to fit smaller wheels, those in the kit being $\frac{1}{16}$ in too great in diameter. Unable to find a pair the correct size I eventually settled for reducing those in the kit by judicious use of wet-and-dry. While on the subject of wheels, those supplied in both the Airfix and Matchbox kits have the solid disc centres, if you want to use the alternative pattern with holed hubs which appeared on several Mosquito variants, it is possible to use the hubs from the Airfix Blenheim kit in the centre of the Mosquito kit wheels although the latter must have their centre drilled out.

The Mk XV version is completed by the addition of a whip aerial in place of the kit aerial part 69, the whip being made from sprue and fitted mid-way between the rear end of the canopy and the fin-rudder.

The original modified aircraft was derived from the bomber version and initially carried the standard dark green/ocean grey/medium grey bomber scheme but was later painted PRU blue over-all. It was also finished in a deep Sky over-all scheme as were the other four versions which served with 85 Squadron, the latter aircraft were painted matt black between March and September 1943 before reverting to the deep Sky camouflage. The serial numbers for these four aircraft were DZ366, DZ385, DZ409 and DZ417, standard roundels and fin flashes for the period were carried and the serials were in black or red.

Bombers and PR Mosquitoes

The Mark IV Bomber is a must for any 1:72 scale collection and unless the old Frog kit is obtained and improved in outline as previously described, there is no alternative other than a conversion.

Before the Matchbox kit was available this conversion involved the moulding of a new nose but it is now possible to use that supplied in the Matchbox kit married to the Airfix fuselage.

The M IV had a clear Perspex nose with small side windows, so parts 29 to 33 from the Matchbox kit are assembled and then cemented in place on the Airfix fuselage after the original nose section has been shortened by cutting it off forward of the wing root leading edge. The crew entry hatch is scribed under the nose and a hole drilled just aft of this and to port of the centre line, to accept the trailing aerial cuff. The pointed windscreen canopy must be fitted complete with the side blisters but with the top moulded blister removed. This is where the Frog canopy comes in particularly useful if you are lucky enough to find one in the spares box, since it does not have the top blister moulded to it. The rest of the Airfix kit is assembled as per instruction using the shrouded exhausts, standard propeller blades and no underwing stores. But remember the Mk IV could carry 50-gallon wing tanks so these can be fitted if the subject chosen is shown, by your research, to have carried them. This version of the bomber can also be constructed from the Matchbox kit by using the Airfix wings and engines married to it. By doing this you will obtain a spare set of wings and stage two Merlins which could for example be matched to the Airfix fuselage, fitted with the Matchbox Universal nose, to produce a Mk XVI.

As the size of the Mosquito's bomb load and the associate weapons increased, it became necessary to fit what was known as the bulged bomb-bay. This was first fitted to a Mk IV in June 1943 and subsequently featured on many bomber and PR aircraft.

There are many ways to make a bulged bomb-bay for the whole range of available kits and the individual must decide which is most suited to his particular skills. Although it is dangerous to generalise, my own personal feelings are that a carved balsa addition is best for 1:72 scale models while a moulded bomb-bay is better in larger scales.

Below left *The additions to the wings are very evident in this view of the NF XV.*

Below right *A PR XVI converted from the Airfix kit using parts from Matchbox for the engines and Frog/Novo for the canopy and nose glazing. Markings are from ESCI sheet No 37 for a 680 Squadron aircraft.*

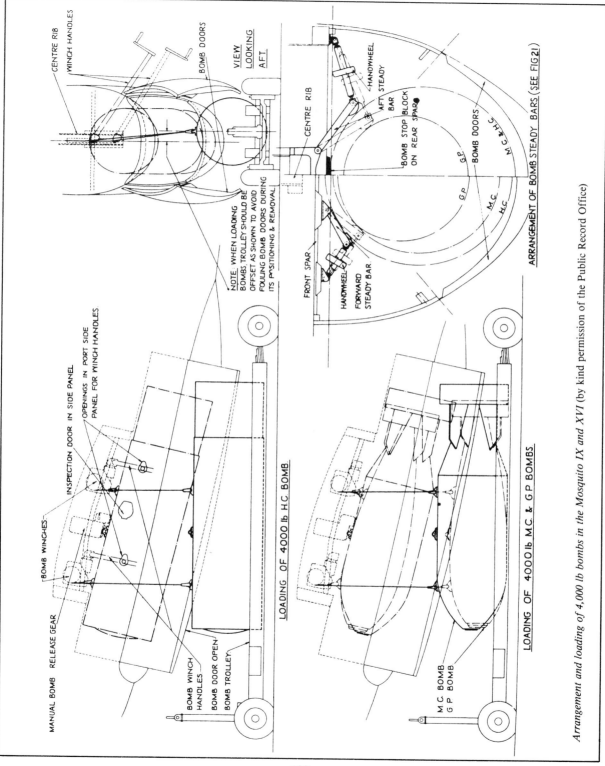

Arrangement and loading of 4,000 lb bombs in the Mosquito IX and XVI (by kind permission of the Public Record Office)

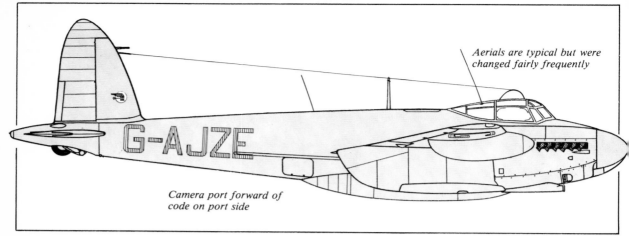

A PR 34 used by RAE Cranfield for gust research and flown by BEA crews. Silver dope over-all with a maroon registration which also appears full span on the top and bottom wing surfaces, G-A to port and JZE to starboard.

The model I have chosen to illustrate this particular feature of the Mosquito is one which started life as a B 35 and after the war was used by the MoS for gust research at Cranfield. There were, in fact, two aircraft used and both were flown by ex-Mosquito crews serving with British European Airways and seconded to the MoS for this duty. The aircraft selected was registered G-AJZE which it carried in red on its silver doped fuselage sides and underneath its mainplanes; the G-A being under the starboard wing and, JZE under the port. The aircraft also carried the BEA 'Flying Key' badge on its fin and port side fuselage nose just below the cockpit.

To construct this model, which can, of course, also be completed as a B 35 or a PR 34, the clear glazed nose from the Matchbox kit is attached to the Airfix fuselage which is assembled in the normal way. When it is dry, remove the bomb-bay along the lines marked on the fuselage moulding using a pointed No 11 blade to make a precise and clean cut. Take a block of soft balsa 2¾ in long and cut the top of it so that it recesses into the area removed, cement this in place and let it set really hard before carving it to the shape required. The rear end of

the block extends over the back end of the bomb bay and it is essential that this area fits flush to the original fuselage undersurface. Once the rough shape has been achieved, use lighter grades of glass-paper to achieve a smooth finish then either paint the balsa with grain filler, or cover the area with a thin coat of Milliput using this also to fill any gaps where the wooden plug and plastic fuselage meet. On larger scale kits the same method is used but the plug removed after shaping to form the mould from which a plastic bay can be produced.

Another method I experimented with which worked reasonably well, was to assemble the fuselage according to the kit instructions, then cement progressively thicker strips of sprue to the bomb-bay area and build up the shape of the bulged bay with Milliput on these. This worked satisfactorily but it requires a lot of work especially when the final shape has been achieved and small areas of imperfections need constant attention before painting can take place. Fit the two-stage Merlins and wings from the Matchbox kit using paddle-bladed propellers from the Airfix offering, six-stack open exhausts are used and the wings have long-range tanks

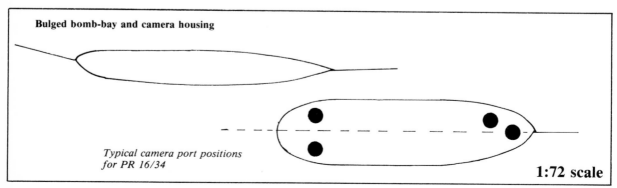

Bulged bomb-bay and camera housing

Typical camera port positions for PR 16/34

1:72 scale

Above and above right *Detail shots like this make work easy when it comes to adding extra detail on large-scale kits. This is the crew entry door on the B 35 currently in the Mosquito Museum at Salisbury Hall.*

Right *Undercarriage detail of the B 35 at Salisbury Hall.*

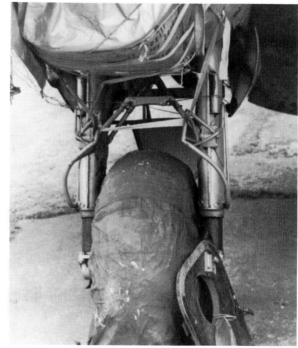

Below *This is the tailwheel assembly of the B 35. The guard in front of the wheel is a legacy from the aircraft's days as a target tug.*

Below right *Undercarriage door detail on the B 35.*

Above *The throttle and pitch lever control box situated on port cockpit side. In this case the aircraft is the B 35 (Stuart Howe).*

Below *Cockpit instrumentation layout in the B 35. Other Mosquitoes were very similar, but remember that fighter versions did not have the spectacle-style control column (Stuart Howe).*

Above *Equipment behind the pilot's seat in a B 35 (Stuart Howe).*

Below *Two 25-gallon fuel tanks in the bomb-bay of a B 35 (Stuart Howe).*

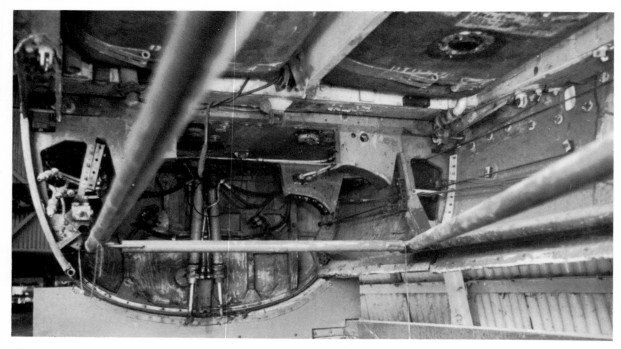

Above and below *Two useful views of the bomb-bay of a B 35 for those interested in super detailing* (Stuart Howe).

Opposite page top *A PR 40 of 87 (PR) Flight RAAF at Coomalie in 1944. The colours are RAAF Azure Blue with the original green camouflage showing through. The serial is white. The diagram is based on a drawing which appeared in IPMS's Australasia magazine.* **Centre** *A PR XVI of 25th Battle Group USAAF at Watton, Norfolk on February 22 1945. It was dark blue over-all with a red tail and black spinners. The wing tank coincides with the black invasion stripe. The blue disc on the tail bears a white S.* **Below** *A PR 34 of 540 Squadron RAF. The colours are PRU blue over-all.*

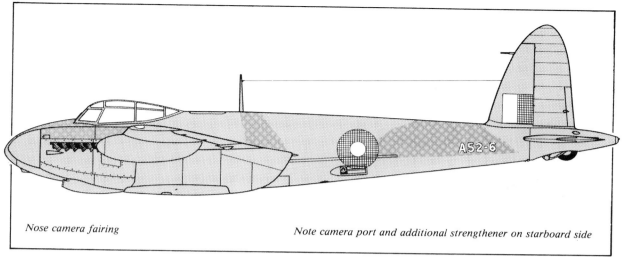

Nose camera fairing

Note camera port and additional strengthener on starboard side

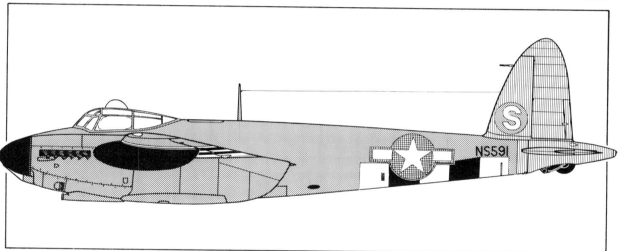

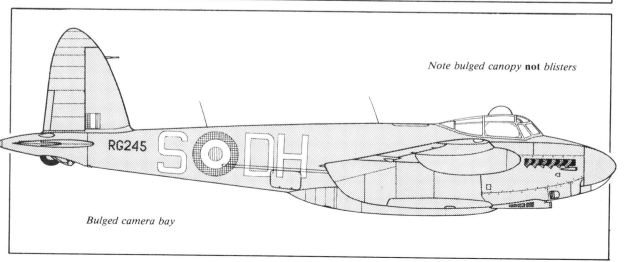

*Note bulged canopy **not** blisters*

Bulged camera bay

The modified PR 34 used at RAE Cranfield for gust research where it was flown by BEA crews. This over-all silver civil registered aircraft makes an unusual addition to any collection of Mosquitoes (British Airways).

fitted. The fuselage is completed by adding the bomber-type canopy minus the side window bulges, but retaining the top blister. The aircraft operated by BEA did at one time have a VHF aerial midway between the canopy and fin/rudder, plus an aerial from just below the fin mounted pitot head to the top of the canopy, and a very long whip aerial protruding from the rear canopy. As previously stated, finish was over-all silver dope, including the spinners, black propellers with yellow tips, and all registration letters in dull red. The BEA badge was red on a white disc and must be hand-painted unless you are lucky enough to find an example from a very early airliner kit which had the original BEA markings as standard. This finish makes a pleasant change from grey/grey/green camouflage, PR blue or all-silver with service markings and is certainly different from the normal camouflaged civil scheme used by BOAC and often chosen by modellers.

The basic conversion can be used for any Marks fitted with bulged bomb- or camera-bays. In models of PR aircraft it is essential that careful research is carried out, as on many of these machines the positions of the camera ports varied and there were often other additions to the airframe, among the latter being the fitting of two external strengthening ribs, the second being attached to the port fuselage side opposite that already standard on the starboard side, a notable example of this being on Australian built PR 41s some of which not only had these two ribs but also a third added just below the port attachment.

These necessarily brief conversion notes have highlighted but a few of the changes to the Mosquito airframe, but they should be enough to sow the seeds for those who are keen to add variety to their modelling. There are many other versions such as the experimental turret Mosquitoes, the Highball machines — which, by the way, were detailed by Gerry Preece in 1976 *Airfix Annual* and are well illustrated in *Mosquito* — the target towing aircraft with weird nose shapes, and naval versions with equally weird noses and fuselages. Clearly it would not be possible to detail all these in a book such as this, indeed it would be unfair to do so, for the joy of modelling is finding out as much as possible for oneself then tackling the conversion in the way best suited to the individual skill and ability. I have merely tried to highlight some of the possibilities and touch on some of the ways the changes can be made, I hope I have helped to point the way and that many readers will be tempted to look further into modelling the many varieties of the wooden wonder.

116

Appendices

1 Useful reference material for the modeller

The following books, articles and magazines, all contain extremely useful material and are strongly recommended to anyone contemplating making a serious attempt at modelling Mosquito variants:

Books

Mosquito, by C. Martin Sharp and Michael J. F. Bowyer (Faber & Faber).

Mosquito at War, by Chaz Bowyer (Ian Allan).

Famous Fighters of WW2, by William Green (Macdonald & Jane's).

Pathfinders at War, by Chaz Bowyer (Ian Allan).

Bomber Squadrons of the RAF, by Philip J. Moyes (MacDonald & Jane's).

Fighter Squadrons of the RAF, by John Rawlings (MacDonald & Jane's).

Mosquito Manual (Arms & Armour Press).

Famous bombers of WW2, by Philip J. Moyes (Hylton Lacy).

Warplanes of the Second World War, by William Green (MacDonald & Jane's).

De Havilland Mosquito, by Francis Mason (Aircam Aviation Series, Vol 28).

Monographs

Profile Publications Nos 52 and 209 (Profile Publications).

Camouflage & Markings No 6 (Ducimus Books).

Camouflage & Markings No 21 (Ducimus Books).

Magazine articles

Airfix Magazine June 1967, July 1968, March 1973, April 1973, November 1973, November 1976.

Scale Models January 1973, August 1974.

Aircraft Illustrated September 1975.

Air International July 1976.

Scale Model Aircraft May 1973.

Scale Modeller August 1979.

There are also numerous articles, colour schemes and drawings in various IPMS publications including the UK, US quarterly and IPMS Australian magazines.

2 Decals

At the time of writing the following specialised decal sheets were available:

1:72 scale

Modeldecal Sheet No 17: Mosquito FB VI 4 Squadron RAF Celle Germany 1946. Microscale Sheet No 72-105:Israeli Air Force Mosquito. ESCI Sheet No 37: PR XVI 680 Squadron.

1:48 scale

Microscale Sheet No 48-13: FB VI of 1 Squadron RAAF, (two aircraft). FB VI of 143 Squadron Coastal Command RAF. FB VI of 415 Squadron RCAF.

3 Kit components

The following table lists the basic components needed for conversions in 1:72 scale and comments about the changes, it is a guide only and should be viewed as such:

Afx = Airfix
MB = Matchbox
BC = Bomber canopy (pointed screen)
FC = Fighter canopy (flat screen)

Mk	Des	Engines	Cockpit	Comments
I	PR	Merlin 21 Afx	BC MB	Short nacelles
II	F/NF	Merlin 21, 22, 23 Afx	FC Afx	
III	T	Merlin 21, 23, 25 Afx	FC Afx	
IV	B	Merlin 21, 23 Afx	BC MB	
VI	FB	Merlin 21, 22, 23, 25, Afx	FC Afx	
VII	B	Merlin 31 MB	BC MB	Canadian-built Mk IV
VIII	PR	Merlin 61 MB	BC MB	
IX	B	Merlin 72/73, 76/77 MB	BC MB	
X	NF	Merlin 61 MB	FC Afx	Not produced
XI	FB	Merlin 61 MB	BC MB	Two-stage equipped; Mk IV not produced
XII	NF	Merlin 21, 23 Afx	FC Afx	Thimble nose
XIII	NF	Merlin 21, 23, 25 Afx	FC Afx	Thimble or Universal nose
XIV	NF	Merlin 67, 72 MB	FC Afx	Two-stage equipped; Mk XIII not produced

Mark	Role	Engine	Code	Notes
XV	NF	Merlin 61, 73, 77 MB	BC MB	Increased span
XVI	PR	Merlin 71/72, 76/77 MB	BC MB	
XVI	B	Merlin 71/72, 76/77 MB	BC MB	Bulged bomb-bay on some aircraft. Overall length 40 ft 6 in
XVII	NF	Merlin 21, 23 Afx	FC Afx	
XVIII	FB	Merlin 25 Afx	FC Afx	
XIX	NF	Merlin 25 Afx	FC Afx	
XX	B	Packard Merlin 31, 33 MB	BC MB	Canadian version of B IV
21	FB	Packard Merlin 31 MB	FC Afx	Canadian version of FB VI
22	T	Packard Merlin 33 MB	FC Afx	Canadian T III
23	B	Packard Merlin 69 MB	BC MB	Canadian-built B IX
24	FB	High altitude version of FB 21 not built		
25	B	Packard Merlin 225 Afx	BC MB	Canadian version of B IV
26	FB	Packard Merlin 225 Afx	FC Afx	
27	T	Packard Merlin 225 Afx	FC Afx	
28		Not used		
29	T	Packard Merlin 225 Afx	FC Afx	All converted T 22
30	NF	Merlin 72, 76 MB	FC Afx	Universal nose
31	NF	Proposed NF 30 with Packard Merlin 69		
32	PR	Merlin 113/114 MB	BC MB	Span increased to 59 ft 2 in
33	TF/TR	Merlin 25 Afx	FC Afx	Fuselage length 42 ft 3 in. Changes include, folding wings, four-bladed props, revised u/c, arrestor hook and reinforced fuselage
34	PR	Merlin 114 MB	BC MB	Bulged Bay
35	B	Merlin 113/114 MB	BC MB	Bulged Bay
36	NF	Merlin 113/114 MB	FC Afx	Universal nose
37	TF	Merlin 25 Afx	FC Afx	Similar to Mk 33
38	NF	Merlin 114 MB	FC Afx	Universal nose, similar to Mk 36
39	TT	Merlin 72/73 MB	BC MB	Conversion of Mk XVI for RN. Longer fuselage, modified nose
40	FB	Packard Merlin 31, 33 MB	FC Afx	Australian-built similar to B VI
41	PR	Packard Merlin 69 MB	BC MB	Australian-built
42	FB	Packard Merlin 69 MB	FC Afx	
43	T	Packard Merlin 33 MB	FC Afx	

There are many minor changes to lengths and the modeller is warned to be careful when checking these as those recorded in various publications vary a great deal depending on the datum line used, the inclusion or omission of aerials, etc. Most of these changes would be hardly noticeable in 1:72 scale.

4 A Mosquito modeller's aide memoire

1 The prototype Mosquito W4050 originally was painted Training Yellow over-all. Her spinners were black, like the serial number. Type A (blue-white-red) roundels were applied on the fuselage sides and underneath the mainplanes. Type B roundels were painted above the wing tips.

2 W4050 was re-painted in January 1941, her sides and upper surfaces then becoming Dark Green and Dark Earth. Spinners remained black, like the fuselage serial. Roundels were updated to accord with the period. No underwing serials were carried.

3 Production Mosquito 1s were finished over-all in PRU Blue and carried, in Medium Sea Grey, the LY lettering of 1 PRU. Their serial numbers were also Medium Sea Grey. Type B roundels were applied above the wing tips and on the fuselage sides, the fin striping also being blue and red.

4 Bombers converted from the first PR production batch were delivered in a scheme of Dark Green and Dark Earth with Sky under surfaces. At no time was the pattern of the paint scheme on Mosquitoes mirrored on alternative aircraft. Spinners on this first batch were black, like the serial numbers. The GB coding of 105 Squadron was applied in Medium Sea Grey. It was in this scheme that the Mosquito bomber went into action.

5 The first production batch and many examples of the second batch of Mosquito fighters wore the standard rough matt black over-all finish of night fighters. From the start 8 in serial numbers were Dull Red, the same colour as their squadron code letters. Mosquitoes

usually carried squadron letters aft, individual letter forward of the fuselage roundel the letters being applied thus on both sides of the fuselage.

6 The main undercarriage gear of Mosquitoes, and the wheel hubs, were invariably silver.

7 In July 1942 the marking and colouring of the Mosquito IVs radically changed. The upper surfaces became Dark Green and Ocean Grey, although some Mosquitoes were provisionally painted instead in Dark Green and a dark shade of grey approximating to that of the Dark Sea Grey applied to some Blenheims of 2 Group in 1941. Under surfaces were re-painted Medium Sea Grey and spinners were dark or Ocean Grey. Serials remained black, but identity letters were now Sky. This scheme better suited them for low-level operations over the sea and for a few months in the summer of 1942 Mosquito bombers had Sky rear fuselage bands and Sky spinners. This was an attempt to lead the enemy into thinking the aircraft were armed fighters. In the event, these markings made the Mosquitoes too conspicuous, and were removed in the autumn. The 1942 variant of Sky applied to Mosquitoes was the usual quite deep green tone common to so many 2 Group aircraft.

8 Autumn 1942 brought a change in fighter camouflage which was to last until the withdrawal of the Mosquito night fighters in the 1950s. Black had too readily caused the Mosquitoes to be seen as silhouettes on moonlit nights, and the thick black paint reduced the fighter's performance. Now, disruptive areas of Dark Green were applied to the upper surfaces, the remainder of which were Medium Sea Grey. This latter colour extended over the entire remainder of the aircraft. Unit identity letters were Dull Red, serials black although some Dull Red serials were observed from time to time on these night fighters.

9 By 1943 the only all-black Mosquitoes were those in training units wherein this finish continued to be used at least to the end of 1944. An interesting variation to the night fighter scheme was visible on many Mosquitoes of 100 Group. Their under belly areas and wing under surfaces were Night. The termination was usually in an irregular, wavy line low on the fuselage side. Again, there were exceptions, some aircraft having the black carried well up the fuselage sides whilst some did not feature black at all.

10 Most Mosquito XIIs originally had black nose radomes, also a few Mk XVIIs.

11 Exhaust detail always needs attention on any Mosquito model since there was a variety of forms. The small, tapering stack type of the Mk 1 gave way to the broader more cylindrical form known as the 'saxophone' type. This was fitted to Mk IIs, IVs, VIs, XIIs, XVIIs, XIXs, XXs and XXVs engaged upon night operations as well. In theory, day-operated Mosquitoes did not have this anti-glare shielding. Most had five-stack ejector exhaust units. Within these guide lines there were some variations which the modeller needs to watch for. The two-stage Merlin Mosquitoes had uncovered six-stack ejector exhaust units irrespective of

their being operated by day or night the exhausts having special glare prevention design incorporated. Equivalent night fighter Mosquitoes had baffles over the exhaust unit into which were fitted louvres to control the brightness of the efflux.

12 Attention to detail brought the best dividends when attempts were made to improve the performance of leading wartime types of aircraft. With the Mosquito this took the form, early on, of removing the radio mast and fitting whip aerials which were often featured by bombers from late 1942.

13 The earliest half-black bomber Mosquitoes were those used by 109 Squadron which had their aircraft thus painted for the commencement of operations in late 1942.

14 Some Oboe leaders had their aircraft marked, if they were of the black finish, with two narrow white bands which encircled the rear fuselage. It was these aircraft which led many of the 1944 day raids directed against French targets by Bomber Command. Mosquitoes of 105 Squadron in some cases wore dark blue code letters.

15 At the close of hostilities a few Coastal Command Mosquitoes were at long last wearing the standard colour scheme for strike aircraft. Their entire upper surfaces were Ocean Grey whilst lower surfaces were Sky. Code letters were Sky too, serials black. The letters were displayed on the fuselage sides above the mainplanes, and hyphenated thus: KK-S.

16 For the 1944 Normandy invasion Mosquito fighter bombers, ADGB night fighters and the Mosquitoes of 1409 Flight acquired the full black and white AEAF stripes applied to aircraft likely to be involved in the battle area. This did not, however, apply to the Mosquitoes of the two Oboe squadrons. By late 1944 these bands were being carried on the fuselage only and during the winter of 1944-5 were further reduced to be carried only on the fuselage under surfaces.

17 Some late-war Mosquito bombers and some of the later examples of the Mosquito VI — particularly those used by Coastal Command — were fitted with paddle-bladed propellers.

18 Mosquito fuselage serial numbers were usually black, sometimes Dull Red as on Night surfaces and on some Mosquitoes of 100 Group. They were in 8 in high figures which were 5 in wide. Strokes were 1 in thick and applied 1 in apart.

19 Under-wing serials on Mosquitoes in post-war RAF service were normally 30 in high. Individual figures and letters were 18¾ in wide and the strokes 3¾ in wide like the spacing between the serial components. Serials were split by the siting of the drop tanks at Wing Rib 8 and were placed to commence at 18 in to either side of the centre line of the rib.

20 Most experimental Mosquitoes retained standard operational colours and markings. One exception was the naval Mk VI prototype conversion. Its upper surfaces were Dark Slate Grey and Extra Dark Sea Grey, its under surfaces and roughly the lower half of the fuselage being yellow. The usual wartime Types B, C and C1 roundels were applied, the wing under surface roundel having an outer diameter of 32 in, white 16 in and red 12 in. The black fuselage serial was the normal RAF size, but the ROYAL NAVY inscription below was in 4 in characters 2½ in wide and in ½ in strokes with ½ in separation. A yellow letter P was 3 ft in maximum width with its extremities set ½ in from the ½ in wide encircling ring which was merely a black outline on the portion painted on the yellow area.

21 Mosquito upper wing surface Type B roundels had an outer diameter of 54 in. The Dull Red centre had a prescribed diameter of 21½ in. Wartime Mosquitoes rarely had under-wing roundels. The Type C1 fuselage roundels had a yellow ring of 36 in in diameter, Dull Blue of 32 in, white 16 in and Dull Red 12 in. The fuselage roundel was supposed to be sited 54 in aft of the wing root.

22 There were several basic variations in the pattern of application of Night (black) to night bomber Mosquitoes. During the war the fins and rudders of such aircraft were black, but the under surfaces terminated at a horizontal line which was the continuation of the centre datum line of the tailplane. In the camouflaged area of the fuselage above the tailplane the serial number was sometimes applied, in black or red on these aircraft. On some Mosquitoes the fuselage area ahead of the roundel had the black irregularly swept down from the roundel to the wing root. The sides of the fuselage nose were painted black in line with the termination of black on the top of the cowling side panelling. Sometimes the top line of the black curved downwards towards the nose glazing.

23 By the 1950s Mosquito night bombers had acquired a finish of Dark Sea Grey upper and Glossy black Anti-Searchlight under surfaces. The boundary between the grey and black on such aircraft was set as a line parallel to the fuselage centre line and passing through a point ¼ below the fuselage top at the point of its maximum depth. In this case the black was swept up to the fin root. Serials red, later white, were then placed equidistant between the top and the bottom of the fuselage. A scheme was prepared in November 1945 for Tiger Force Mosquitoes in which the grey area was replaced by Matt White.

24 A typical photographic reconnaissance Mosquito of the mid-war period would be PR Blue over-all with 54-in outer diameter Type B upper surface roundels and further Type B fuselage roundels, Blue of 32 in in

diameter and Dull Red of 12.8 in. The fin striping was by then the usual Dull Red-white-Dull Blue and of 12 in in height, like the width. The red and blue stripes were 5 in high. This scheme came into being in April 1944 the fin striping replacing the previously usual red and blue. Only Mosquitoes of 1 PRU carried unit identity letters, but later in the war some PR aircraft carried Medium Sea Grey small individual letters.

25 After the war there were a variety of colour schemes applicable to PR aircraft. Some retained the all-silver finish applied to many such machines in the Far East late in the war. Others retained for many years the over-all PR Blue paintwork. A third colour scheme seen on a number of PR 34s and 34As consisted of Medium Sea Grey upper surfaces and PR Blue under surfaces. Fins and rudders were also PR Blue. On the engine cowling the dividing line followed the top line of the cowling panel. The fuselage dividing line in this case was a straight line between the leading edge of the tailplane and the top of the wing to the fuselage joint in line with the rear of the canopy. Serial numbers on the fuselage were placed one inch above the fuselage dividing line and were black. Roundels were of Type D. The upper wing roundels were 54 in in outer diameter, the white disc being of 36 in and the red 18 in. Fuselage roundels had an outer diameter of 36 in, 24 for the white disc and 12 for the red, these colours including the post-war Bright Red and Bright Blue. Upper wing roundels were centred 18 ft from the fuselage centre line, at the customary one third of half the wing span from the wing tip.

26 Post-war trainer Mosquito T IIIs were painted Aluminium alias silver over-all in a scheme laid down in November 1947. A yellow band 36 in wide, the rear line of which was applied 3 ft 6 in forward of the tailplane, encircled the fuselage. A 3 ft wide yellow band also wrapped around the mainplanes its outer line passing through the outer forward corner of the outer flaps. Unlike bombers and PR aircraft, these trainers had 3 ft diameter under-wing red-white-blue roundels placed so that the forward and centre points of the roundels were 1 in from the wing leading edge and the ailerons respectively.

27 These colours much contrasted with the usual wartime Mosquito T III finish which consisted of Dark Green and Ocean Grey upper surfaces and Medium Sea Grey lower surfaces. Outer wing leading edges had a yellow stripe common to day fighters in the mid-war period. Their spinners were Sky like the band around the rear fuselage.

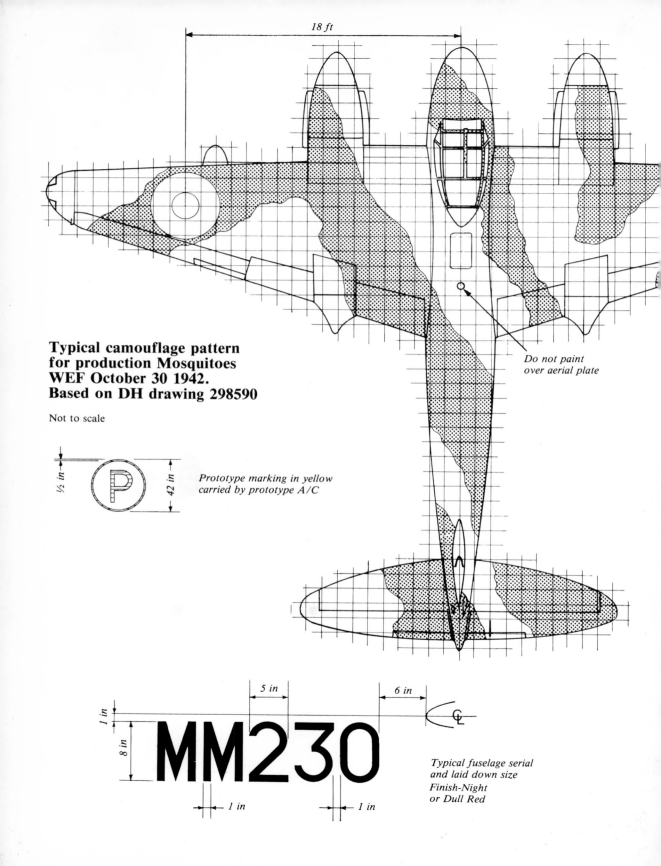

18 ft

**Typical camouflage pattern
for production Mosquitoes
WEF October 30 1942.
Based on DH drawing 298590**

Not to scale

½ in   42 in

*Prototype marking in yellow
carried by prototype A/C*

*Do not paint
over aerial plate*

5 in   6 in

1 in

8 in

MM230

1 in   1 in

*Typical fuselage serial
and laid down size
Finish-Night
or Dull Red*